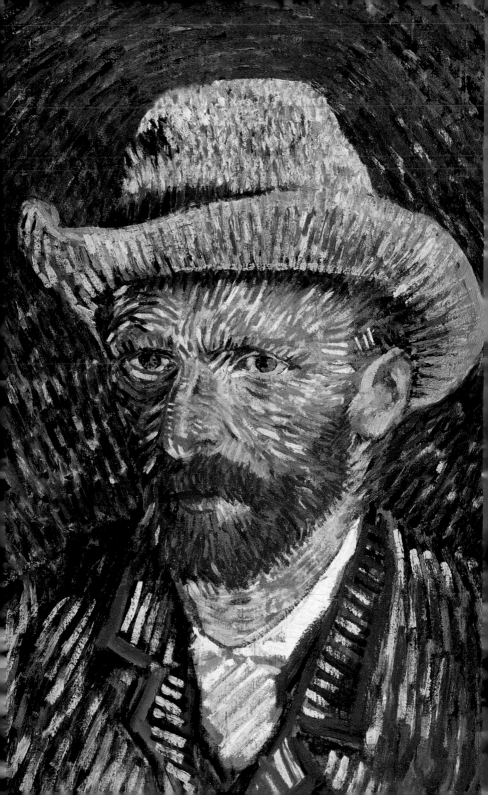

# ArtBook
# Van Gogh

**DORLING KINDERSLEY**
London • New York • Sydney • Moscow
Visit us on the World Wide Web at http://www.dk.com

# Contents

## How to use
## this book

This series presents both the life and works of each artist within the cultural, social, and political context of their time. To make the books easy to consult, they are divided into three areas which are identifiable by side bands: yellow for the pages devoted to the life and works of the artist, light blue for the historical and cultural background, and pink for the analysis of major works. Each spread focuses on a specific theme, with an introductory text and several annotated illustrations. The index section is also illustrated and gives background information on key figures and the location of the artist's works.

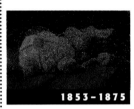

**1853–1875**

### Vincent the Dutchman

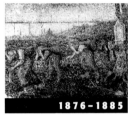

**1876–1885**

### Preaching and poverty

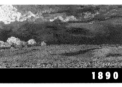

**1890**

### Epilogue

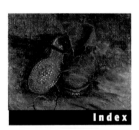

**Index**

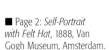

■ Page 2: *Self-Portrait with Felt Hat*, 1888, Van Gogh Museum, Amsterdam.

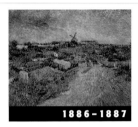

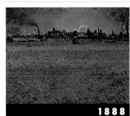

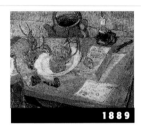

**1886–1887**

**1888**

**1889**

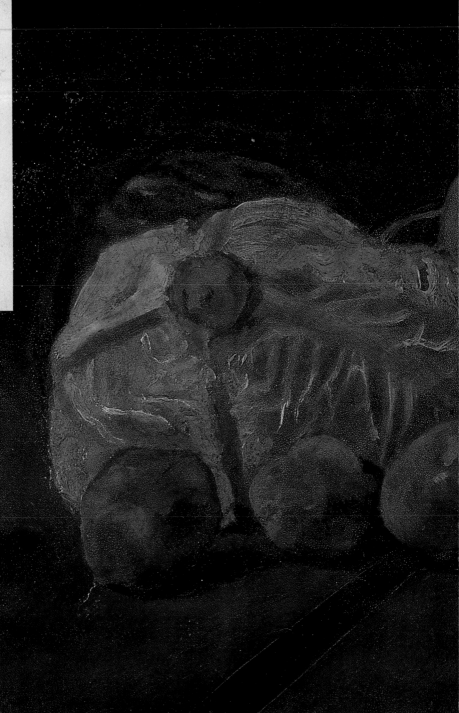

**1853–1875**

# Vincent the Dutchman

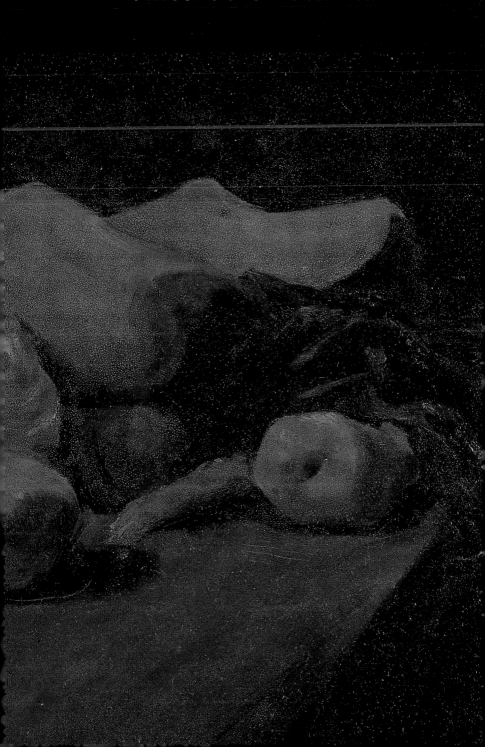

# The preacher's family

**"S**tocky rather than slender, his back curved by letting his head hang limp, his hair cut short under a straw hat meant to shelter his strange-looking face. His forehead was always slightly knitted, his eyebrows frowning from the intense meditation, his small eyes were sometimes blue, sometimes green...". Vincent van Gogh's younger sister Elizabeth has left this portrait of the artist, who was a difficult and unsociable adolescent. The son of Theodorus, a Protestant pastor, and Anna Cornelia Carbentus, Vincent was born on March 30, 1853, in Groot Zundert, a small village in Dutch Brabant. A year earlier to the day, in the same presbytery, Anna had given birth to a still-born child, who had also been christened Vincent. As a consequence of this tragic coincidence, the future artist grew up burdened by a fatal sense of guilt, as if he felt that his life had only been possible because of the sacrifice of another existence. Vincent felt that he had sinned by being born, and his continuous, heartbreaking search for maternal affection was the result of his feeling undeserving of his mother's love for being alive instead of his brother. After Vincent, Anna and Theodorus had five more children: Anna, Theo, Elizabeth, Wilhelmine, and Cornelius. The names Vincent and Theodorus often recurred in the family genealogy. Throughout his life Vincent kept a regular correspondence with Theo and Wilhelmina.

■ Rembrandt, *Burgomaster Six*, 1647. In a letter to Theo, Vincent wrote: "You know the etching by Rembrandt, *Burgomaster Six*, standing reading before a window? I sometimes think that Uncle Vincent and Uncle Cor must have resembled him when they were younger".

■ The small and picturesque church of Zundert, where Vincent and his brother Theo were christened, was built in 1806.

■ Vincent grew up near the parish cemetery where his still-born brother, also named Vincent, was buried. This proximity to death had a profound effect on him, and the sense of this trauma is portrayed in many works. In *Cradle* (right), sketched in a letter to Theo in 1882, the child has nobody to look after him.

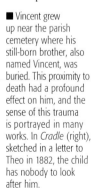

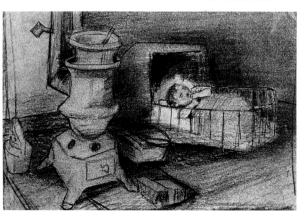

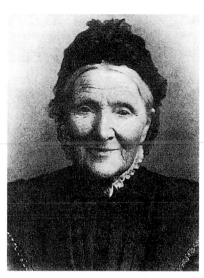

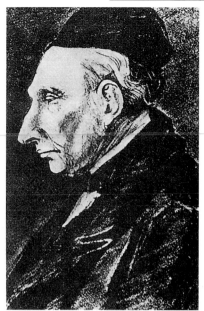

■ Anna Cornelia
Carbentus was born
in 1819, and died in
1907. She loved nature
and the open air, and
had was a great letter
writer. Vincent probably
derived his talents as
a writer from her.

■ Theodorus van Gogh,
Vincent's father, was a
pleasant man, but not
successful as a preacher:
as a result, the
ecclesiastical hierarchy
confined him to poor,
peripheral parishes.
Anna Carbentus, on
the other hand, was a
strong, decisive woman.

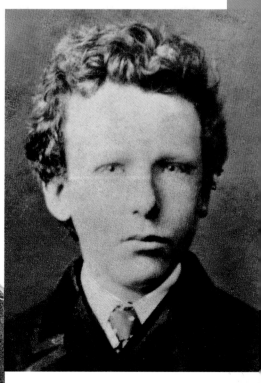

■ Vincent was a lonely
boy, who used to spend
his days walking in the
fields, collecting eggs
and nests. Upon seeing
this photograph, Picasso
commented on the
resemblance with
the young Rimbaud.

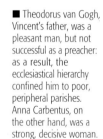

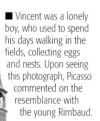

**1853–1875**

# On the fields
# of heather

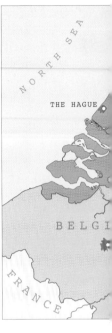

THE HAGUE

BELGI

Bordering with Belgium, Dutch Brabant is a complex area, not least from a religious point of view: although officially part of the Protestant Netherlands, it is heavily influenced by the Catholicism of Flanders. Partly as a result of this religious duality, Vincent's father never had many listeners during his sermons. This increased Vincent's sense of angry impotence, who spent his time exploring the surrounding countryside. The local landscape does not feature conventionally beautiful or impressive scenery: on the contrary, the flat horizon and the subtle tones of grey create an impression of melancholic sobriety that is ideal for a silent, meditative spirit. The moors, the heaths, and the brown earth entered the heart of Vincent van Gogh, who never forgot "the misty air" of his native country. Many years later, in Arles, he wrote, "During my illness I saw again every room in the house at Zundert, every path, every plant in the garden, the views of the fields, the neighbors, the graveyard, the church, and our kitchen garden at the back …". In 1865, Vincent went to study in nearby Zavenburgen, but he was an absent-minded student, and he was desperately homesick. The first separation from his family had a profound mark on his psychological development.

■ Northern Brabant is bounded by the Belgian border and the lower course of the Meuse. Its capital is 's-Hertogenbosch, where painter Hieronymus Bosch was born.

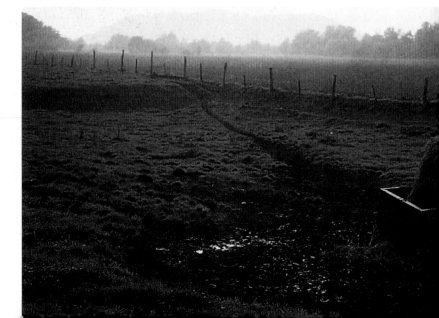

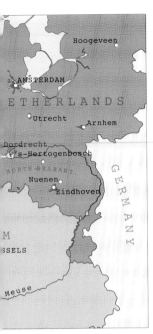

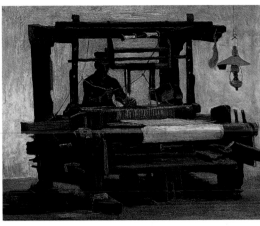

■ *The Weaver*, 1884, Kröller-Müller Museum, Otterlo. Since the 1400s, Brabant had been known for its cloth production. In 1884 Vincent portrayed the hard work of the weavers, whose mechanical movements fascinated him. He felt they had "a dreamy expression", and described this scene in a letter, writing that the "colossal black thing" had a gloomy aspect and the color of an old oak tree.

■ Van Gogh was born here, but his original home was destroyed in 1903. His birthplace is marked by a plaque bearing one of his famous phrases: "I feel that my work has its roots in the heart of the people".

■ The Dutch landscape, characterized by mists and flat horizons, always had a place in Vincent's heart. Before dying, he tried to return to his homeland.

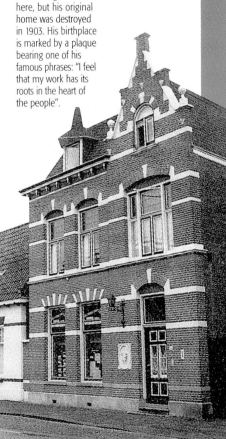

# An inner light

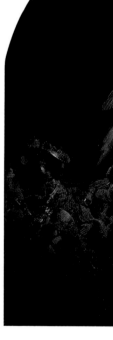

■ Rembrandt, *The Resurrection of Christ*, 1639, Alte Pinakothek, Munich. Painted for the stadtholder Frederick Henry of Orange, this masterpiece was executed with visionary genius.

In order to understand van Gogh's character, one must be aware of the ties that bound him to the culture of his native land. Several aspects recur throughout the history of Dutch painting. One of these distinctive traits is the search for simplicity and honesty, the rejection of any intellectualizing tendency. Another feature is the belief in the moral significance of art, which should not idealize reality, but find in it a sacredness, even in everyday events and objects. Van Gogh had studied art, and knew that the great Dutch masters of the 17th century had respected these theories. In particular, he was impressed by the art of Rembrandt (1606–69), whose works were characterized by a profound humanity, and perfectly captured both drama and tenderness. He admired the way Rembrandt used the interplay of light and shade to such dramatic effect, his truth to nature in portraiture, "though even there, he soars aloft, to the very highest height, the infinite", and his poetic manipulation of the medium when "he was free to idealize". In October 1885, after seeing *The Night Watch* and *The Jewish Bride* in the Rijksmuseum, Vincent wrote to Theo: "He must have died several times to be able to paint like that".

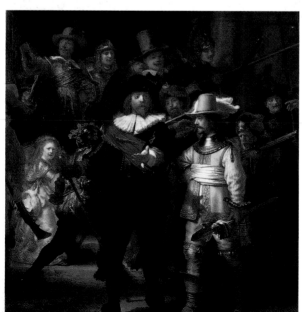

■ Rembrandt, *The Night Watch*, 1642, Rijksmuseum, Amsterdam. In this masterpiece of Baroque complexity, Rembrandt inserted both realistic and symbolic elements. Movement, light, and color are successfully integrated thanks to the intricate chiaroscuro effects.

■ Rembrandt, *The Entombment of Christ*, 1639, Alte Pinakothek, Munich. Guided by a touching compassion, the characters seem to emerge from the shadow and move toward Christ's luminous body.

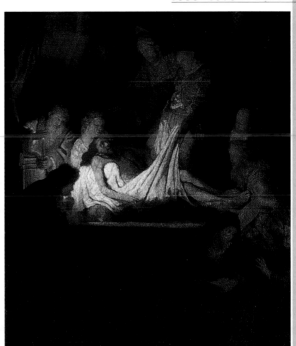

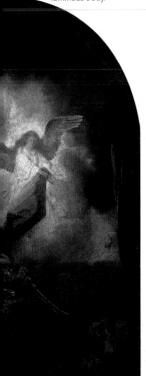

■ Rembrandt, *The Descent from the Cross*, 1633, Alte Pinakothek, Munich. This work was inspired by the painting of the deposition that Rubens had created some 20 years before for Antwerp cathedral.

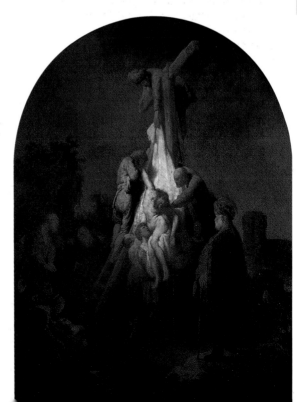

# The picture trade

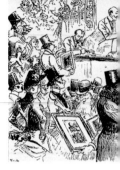

When he turned 16, Vincent van Gogh had to make his first professional choice: although he did not yet feel a vocation for a specific career, his family was large and in need of financial help. On July 30, 1869, his uncle Vincent, a successful art dealer, found him a position as a clerk in the Hague branch of the Parisian Maison Goupil under the supervision of H.G. Tersteeg. Just like Gauguin, who was working as a bank clerk in Paris at about the same time, Vincent was the ideal employee. His enthusiasm for the subject earned him an excellent reference and in June 1873 he was transferred to the London branch. Although Vincent would later criticise the art trade, the experience enabled him to discover more about the commercial art world and exposed him to a broad range of fine art imagery. At the time, the Hague branch of the Goupil group was responsible for selling paintings, as well as producing and selling etchings, lithographs, and prints. The diffusion of the latter meant that art was no longer a privilege of the upper classes, but also became accessible to the bourgeoisie.

■ Robida, *À L'Hôtel des Ventes*, drawing published in *La Caricature*, 1887. This print is a lively testimony of a gathering of painters and dealers at an art sale. Lithographs and prints immediately created a market for art reproductions.

■ William Bouguereau (1825–1905) was one of the main exponents of academic art, and his works attracted attention at many Salons. He was Napoleon III's official painter, and his cold interpretations of mythological scenes made him a despised enemy of the Impressionists. Vincent was familiar with many of his works.

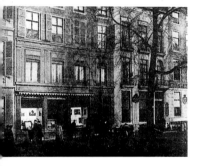

■ In the photograph above is Goupil Auction House in Plaats 14, The Hague. Founded in 1827, within just over 30 years the Goupil group had a virtual monopoly on artistic reproductions. Here Vincent saw many copies of masterpieces, from paintings of the Barbizon School, to works by Boldini, Millet, and Meissonier. The engraver Luigi Calamatta also worked for Goupil.

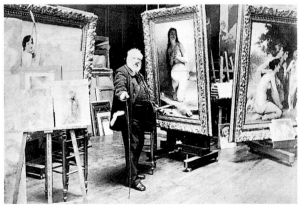

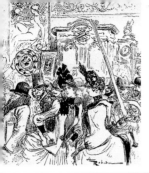

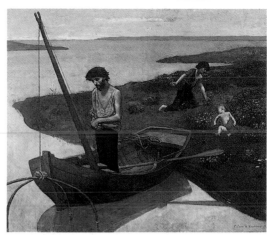

■ Pierre Puvis de Chavannes, *The Poor Fisherman*, 1881, Musée d'Orsay, Paris. For Vincent, the fisherman in this allegorical work represented the life of simple people.

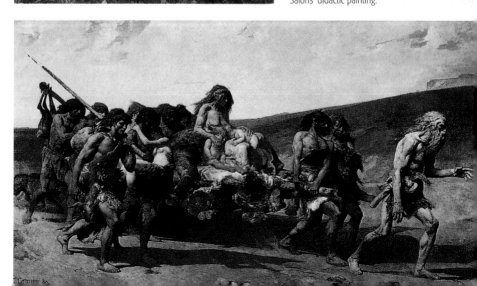

■ James Ensor, *Afternoon in Ostend*, 1881, Koninklijk Museum voor Schone Kunsten, Antwerp. Ensor's early paintings of bourgeois interiors, later gave way to the macabre imaginings for which he is chiefly known.

■ Fernand Cormon, *Cain*, 1880, Musée d'Orsay, Paris. Illustrative of Cormon's masterly technique, this work features an unlikely subject, typical of the Salons' didactic painting.

# The Hague School

In about 1870, several painters from different areas of the Netherlands gathered in The Hague. The city, lying about 6.4 kilometers (4 miles) from the North Sea, was surrounded by dunes that have now disappeared under recent buildings; nearby was the fishing village of Scheveningen, now a crowded tourist resort. Eager to pay tribute to the Old Dutch Masters, these artists were especially interested in landscape painting, although some of them focused their attention on the everyday lives of peasants, which they portrayed with a nostalgic tone and an underlying feeling of humble resignation. At this time, Vincent was living with his great-aunt Sophy, whose daughter was engaged to Anton Mauve, a leading member of The Hague School. Mauve used an almost photographic style to paint delicate subjects, and adopted the subdued palette of the Flemish painters, which suited his austere moral message. The young van Gogh was in need of a hero to look up to and, for a some time, he admired and worshipped Mauve. The main protagonists of The Hague School, Anton Mauve, the Maris brothers, and Joszef Israëls, created a sort of artist's society. Named the Pulchri Studio, the group met regularly to discuss art and following Manet's example, attempted to make painting more relevant and contemporary. During the spring of 1882, van Gogh himself joined this group, where he met Willem Maris and George Breitner. He wrote of Israëls' art: "His figures have a soul".

■ Joszef Israëls,
*A Son of the Old Folk*,
1883, Rijksmuseum,
Amsterdam. Israëls was
extremely popular in
his day. He specialized
in scenes from daily life
and, as in this example,
monuments and
characters from
the Jewish ghetto.

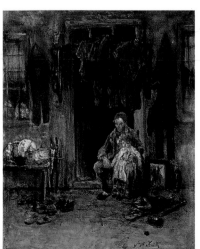

■ *Peach Tree*
*in Blossom*, 1888,
Kröller-Müller Museum,
Otterlo. When Mauve
died, van Gogh sent
this work to his widow.

■ Anton Mauve,
*Fishing Boat on the*
*Beach*, 1882, Haags
Gemeentemuseum,
The Hague. Mauve's
influence is evident in
van Gogh's first sketches
from the Etten period.

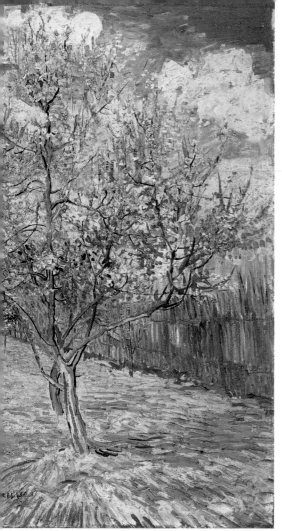

■ Anton Mauve, *Self-Portrait*, 1884, Haags Gemeentemuseum, The Hague. Like van Gogh, Mauve was the son of a Protestant pastor. Although by no means exclusive, his artistic influence on van Gogh was remarkable.

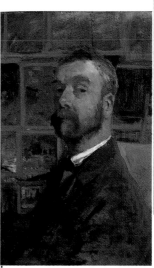

## Anton Mauve

Considered by his contemporaries one of the most modern artists of his time, Anton Mauve was related to the van Gogh family through his wife, Jet Carbentus, who was a cousin of Vincent's mother. His paintings often portray the Dutch countryside or the beach of Scheveningen, which he rendered with delicate, sensitive touches of grey and silver. When taking his first steps into the art world, van Gogh worshipped Mauve; however their rapport became tense in 1882, when Anton, ill, refused to see him. When Theo told him about Mauve's death, Vincent dedicated his *Peach Tree in Blossom* to him.

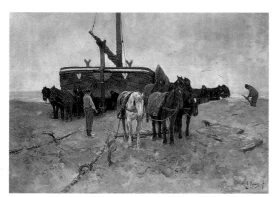

# Dickens' London

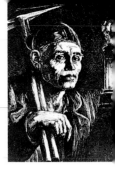

I n 1873, the Goupil Art Gallery sent Vincent to London, while Theo, who had been employed shortly after his brother, was transferred to the Brussels branch. Vincent was happy to be in the city he had discovered in Dickens' novels. He enjoyed walking along the Thames, sketching portraits of passers-by; and spent his weekends in museums, where he became familiar with British painting. He also kept an album, which he filled with passages of prose and poems that had particularly moved him. In this solitude, he fell in love with Eugenie Loyer, his landlady's daughter. Once again, his search for love was colored by his family history and his need to be validated by maternal affection. His love was unrequited, and the disappointment started a sequence of self-punishing acts. He visited his parents, who had moved to Etten, but his state of mind was the cause of constant rows. He returned briefly to London, but was rejected again and transferred to the Parisian headquarters of Maison Goupil. His relationship with those around him deteriorated further, until it began to affect his job: in April 1876, he was dismissed. He was by now convinced of his religious calling and increasingly sought solice in the Bible. In early 1877 he returned to Holland, where he found a job as a bookseller in Dordrecht.

■ Matthew White Ridley, *Portraits of the People: The Miner*, 1876. Vincent wrote to Theo saying that English engravers chose subjects as real as those by Gavarni and Daumier, but noted there was a nobility about them, and that they were executed with a "serious tone".

■ Luke Fildes, *Hungry and Homeless*, 1877. Such scenes of urban, working-class society deeply disturbed the young van Gogh and influenced his own choice of subjects.

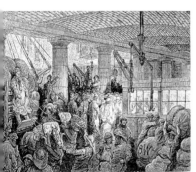

■ Gustave Doré, *St Katharine's Dock* from *Travels to London* (1872). This book was the first to report on the conditions of workers in an industrial city.

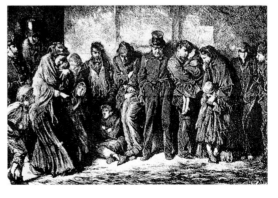

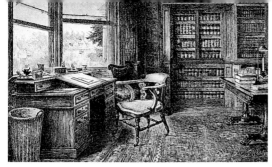

■ Luke Fildes, *The Empty Chair, Gad's Hill, 9 June, 1870*. This engraving of Charles Dickens' empty chair, purchased by van Gogh, was created by Fildes in commemoration of the great author.

■ *Still Life with Open Bible, Candlestick, and Novel*, 1885, Van Gogh Museum, Amsterdam. The placing of a well-thumbed copy Emile Zola's *La Joie de Vivre* alongside his father's Bible is indicative of Vincent's passion for literature.

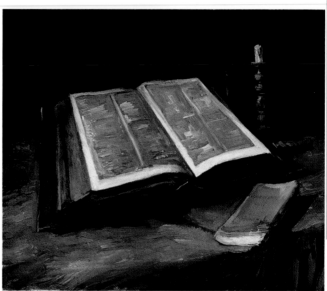

■ John Constable, *The Cornfield*, 1826, National Gallery, London. While in London, Vincent visited many galleries and museums. He wrote enthusiastically to Theo about works by Constable and Turner.

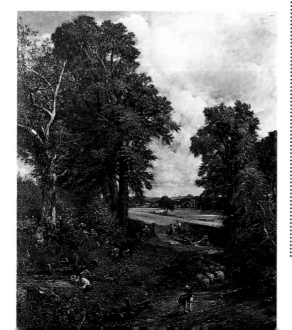

## Vincent and literature

Vincent van Gogh thought that love for literature was "sacred", just like love for art. From a young age, he memorized long passages by Harriet Beecher Stowe and Dickens. In London he read Keats, Eliot, Hugo, and Renan. Soon after, the Bible became his exclusive reading matter. In the mid-1880s, he discovered Zola and the Goncourt brothers, as well as serial stories by Octave Feuillet and Richepin. A great admirer of Loti, he also respected the work of Honoré de Balzac, but was indifferent to Mallarmé's obscure symbolism. He also loved Greek tragedies.

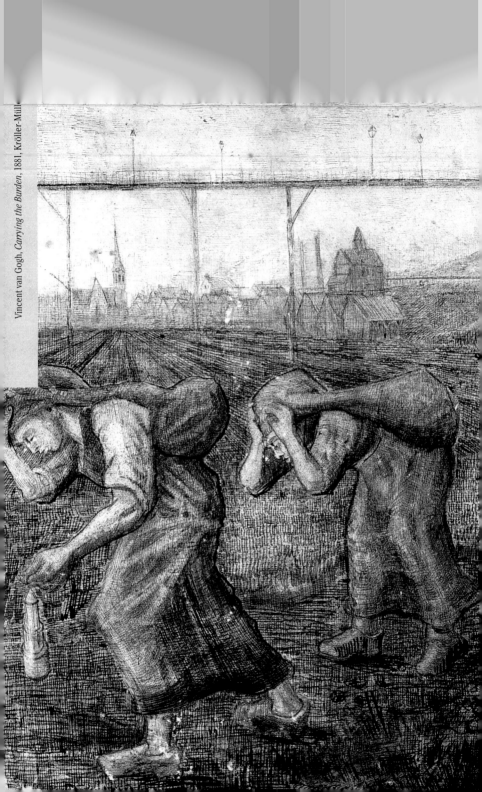

# Preaching and poverty

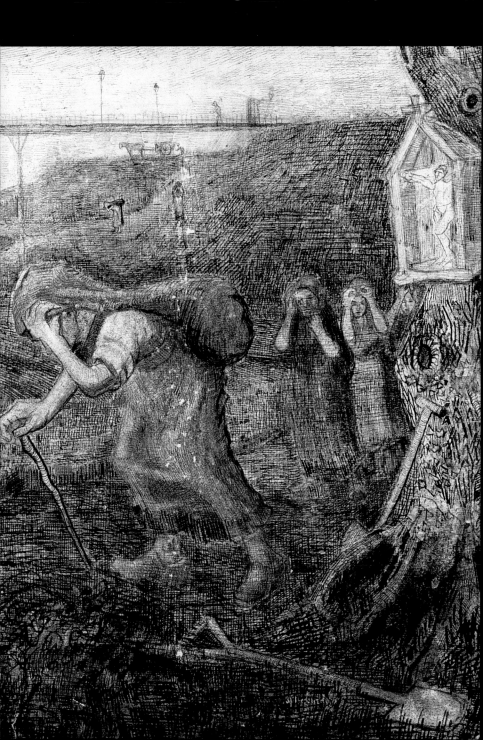

**1876-1885**

# A feeling of worthlessness...

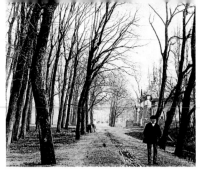

For a few months Vincent worked as an assistant in a bookshop in Dordrecht. There he attended services at churches of several denominations and spent much of his time transcribing passages from the Bible. In May 1877, having persuaded his parents of the seriousness of his religious calling, he enrolled in a Protestant theology course at the University of Amsterdam. His uncle Jan gave him a room, and his mother's brother, pastor Stricker, helped him with his studies. One of his tutors was a young man of Jewish origins, Mendes da Costa. In spite of all the attention lavished on Vincent, his results were not encouraging, especially since he felt that Greek and Latin were completely removed from his experience. However, he was impressed with the devotion to life expressed in Thomas à Kempis' *The Imitation of Christ*. Da Costa wrote: "I used to see him arrive from my room on the third floor. He would have his books under his right arm and, in the left hand, a bunch of snowdrops he had just picked up". Van Gogh derived more joy from walking along the canals or through the former ghetto where Rembrandt used to live.

■ Oosterburgraafplats, Oosterpark, Amsterdam. "After the sermon, I walked along the station all the way to the cemetery, on a path of black ash cutting through the fields: they looked beautiful in the twilight."

■ Above is Vincent's certificate of enrolment from the Academy of Fine Arts in Antwerp. He enrolled at the Academy in 1886, thereby ending his career as a preacher. Soon, in spite of his desire to improve, he spoke out against the absurd bureaucracy of the system, and argued with his teachers. He subsequently decided to move to Paris.

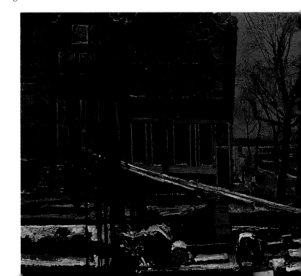

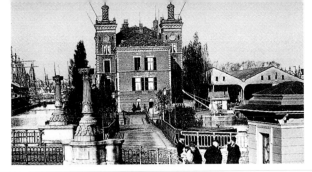

■ This photograph portrays the *Marinewerf*, home of the Amsterdam harbor master in 1890. Vincent was a less than enthusiastic student and often wandered around the city. He would have been familiar with the habor and dockyard.

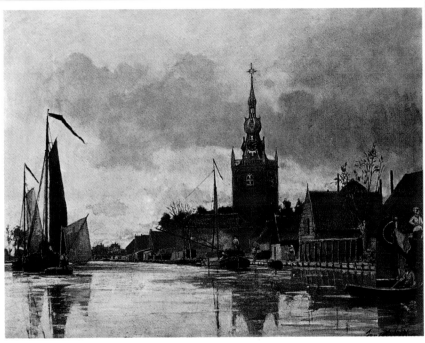

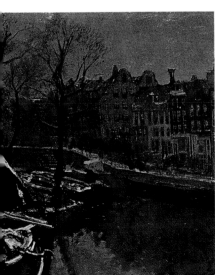

■ Johan Barthold Jongkind, *Overschir*, 1856, Musée des Beaux-Arts, Douai, France. The Dutch artist Jongkind created the most accurate portrayals of 19th-century Amsterdam. His research into the effects light anticipated some Impressionist techniques.

■ George Hendrik Breitner, *View of Laurinergracht*, 1895, Stedelijk Museum, Amsterdam. Breitner began his career painting circular "panoramas", which were exhibited in many tourist resorts. He is better known for his realistic renderings of Amsterdam, its harbor and bustling streets.

# Seeing the sorrow
of men

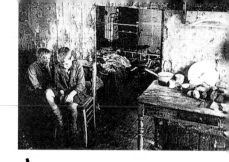

■ Georges Minne, *Man Mourning a Dead Doe*, 1896, Museum voor Schone Kunsten, Gand. The Belgian socialist sculptor Minne gave a symbolic depth to Meunier's naturalism; he also denounced the horrific working and living conditions of the miners. In this sculpture, the crouching figure resembles those trapped in the lava in the disaster of Pompeii.

After abandoning his studies, Vincent went to Laecken, near Brussels, where he trained as a lay preacher. He left three months later, on November 15, 1878, and found a job in the mining district of Borinage, one of the most impoverished areas in Belgium. Vincent arrived as a lay preacher in Wasmes, near Mons: it was a mining community plagued by epidemics, poverty, and unsafe working conditions. Eager to share the suffering of the miners, he gave them everything he owned, and even cut his own clothes in half. His behavior aroused surprise, sometimes even mistrust: when he was reported to the authorities, the inspector justified the preacher's antics as mystic madness. Theo disapproved of his brother's choices, and Vincent stopped writing to him for nine months. He was obsessed with Fyodor Dostoyevsky's Prince Miskin, a character from *The Idiot*, and the need to annihilate oneself completely in order to find the true self. Then, in July 1880, after Theo sent him 50 francs, their letters resumed. In October 1880, he moved to Brussels to indulge his new passion: becoming an artist.

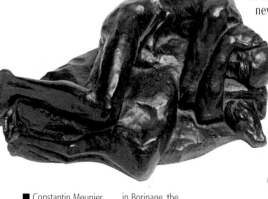

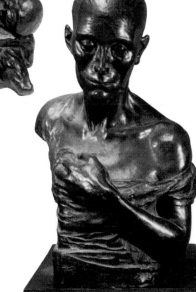

■ Constantin Meunier, *Woman of the Folk*, c.1890, Koninklijk Museum voor Schone Kunsten, Antwerp. The poor living conditions of the depressed mining communities in Borinage, the firedamp explosions, and the appalling exploitation of workers were described in Emile Verhaeren's poems, and portrayed in Meunier's tragic bronze statues.

■ This is a still from the 1933 documentary *Borinage*, by Joris Ivens and Henry Storck. Remembering Vincent, Ivens declared: "The cine-camera voiced our indignation", and "Every honest artist who saw this became a different man".

■ Below is an image from the 1934 film *New Land Zuidersee*, by Joris Ivens. This is another socially important document inspired by van Gogh's writings. The music for the film was composed by Hans Eisler.

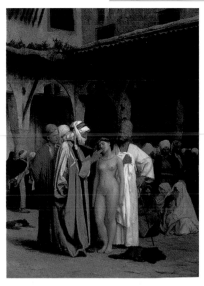

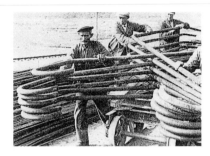

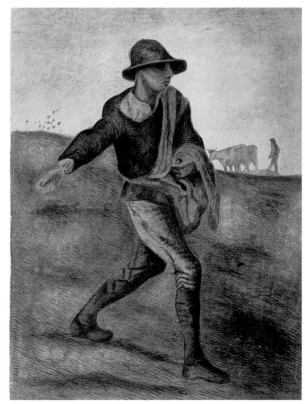

■ Jean-Léon Gérôme, *The Slave Market*, 1866, Clark Institute, Williamstown. Inspired by Gérard de Nerval's *Voyage en Orient* (1843–51), this work was a great success. Vincent's uncle Cornelius asked him if he would like a woman like the one in the picture, but the artist said that he would prefer "one who, through experience and sorrow, had gained a mind and soul.

■ *The Sower* (after Millet), April 1881, Van Gogh Museum, Amsterdam. A subject close to van Gogh's heart, the sower is the symbol of a laborious country life, but also a reference to the parables of the Gospel. Vincent considered preaching to be the "sowing of the Word".

**1876–1885**

# First artistic attempts

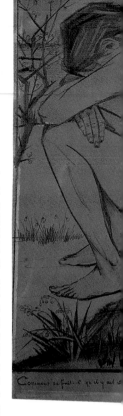

Vincent arrived in Brussels on October 15, 1880. Here he met Anton van Rappard (1858–92), a student at the Académie des Beaux-Arts, who welcomed him in his studio and taught him the rules of perspective. Although there seemed to be nothing in common between the aristocratic van Rappard and Vincent, they were friends for five years. Van Gogh studied anatomy, copied his favorite reproductions, and portrayed his experiences in Borinage. He missed his parents, however, and, on April 12, 1881, he returned to Etten. In this period he focused exclusively on drawings, in which he rendered the mundane reality of people's lives, the places and tools of their work. In December 1881, he went to The Hague, where his cousin by marriage Anton Mauve, a specialist in the rustic genre, looked after him. He began a relationship with Sien Hoornik, who had a child and was expecting another when Vincent met her. When the baby was born, van Gogh put great energy into preparing a new room. The baby touched him, and he wrote of the intense feeling of a man seated beside the woman he loves, with an infant child in the cradle next to them. Sien posed for about 60 drawings and watercolors. On September 11, 1883, Vincent went to Drenthe, in the north of the Netherlands.

■ *Beach at Scheveningen in Stormy Weather*, August 1882, Vincent Van Gogh Museum, Amsterdam.

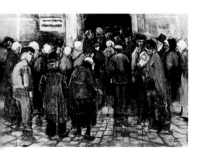

■ *The State Lottery Office*, September 1882, Van Gogh Museum, Amsterdam. At the time of this work, Vincent wrote that he felt a great creative force, and that one day he would be able to create good material regularly.

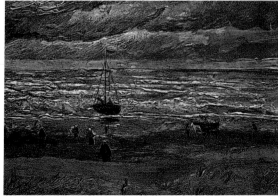

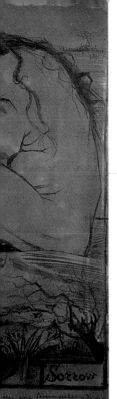

## Vincent and women

In a letter to his brother Theo in 1882, Vincent wrote that he knew why Michelet said, "Women are a religion". Rejected by Eugenie Loyer during his stay in London, then by his cousin Kee Vos (née Stricker), whose refusal led him to burn himself with a candle until he fainted, Vincent dreamed of a mother figure. In his lonely life, an important role was played by prostitutes, from Sien to Rachel, to whom he sent his ear after the row with Gauguin in December 1888. Vincent was attracted to the sadness of physical degradation, which he felt enveloped people close to his own suffering. Sien's face was marked by smallpox, and she suffered from venereal diseases. Vincent wrote that he and Sien were two unhappy souls keeping each other company and carrying their burden together.

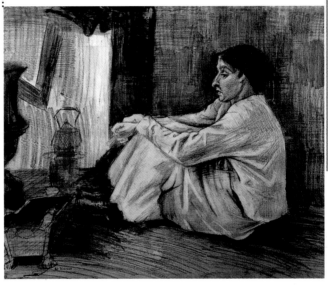

■ *Sorrow*, 1882, Walsall Museum & Art Gallery. This poignant sketch of Sien shows her wretched state when Vincent found her, pregnant and alone.

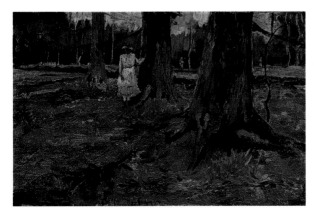

■ *Sien with a Cigar, Sitting on the Floor by the Hearth*, 1882, Kröller-Müller Museum, Otterlo. In this sketch, Sien is invested with a great, tragic strength.

■ *A girl in the Wood*, 1882, Kröller-Müller Museum, Otterlo. This is the first version of a recurring subject: huge trees and a minute figure dwarfed by their magnitude.

27

# Nuenen

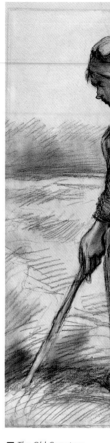

Although initially attracted by the remote moors of Drenthe, the lonliness and isolation were too much for Vincent. He stopped in Hoogeveen, then returned to his parents, who had moved to Nuenen, a Catholic town east of Breda, near Eindhoven. He stayed there until November 1885: during this period his models were farmers and weavers. At about this time, Vincent tried to persuade Theo to become an artist and give up art dealing. He did this in an enthusiastic letter in which he invited his brother to join him on the moors and in his observations of rural life: "come and... look into the fire with me". Vincent's father died on March 26, 1885 and, as he tried to paint the graveyard where he was buried, the artist wrote about his desire to express the simplicity of death and burial. He felt they were as simple as "the falling of an autumn leaf". And again: "A stumpy old tower in a little churchyard with an earth bank and a beech hedge, the flat scenery of heath or cornfields... everything was exactly like the most beautiful Corots. A stillness, a mystery, a peace as only he has painted it...". On November 24, 1885, Vincent moved to Antwerp, where he studied the works of Peter Paul Rubens and enrolled at the Academy of Fine Arts. However, he soon moved to Paris.

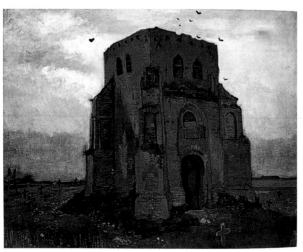

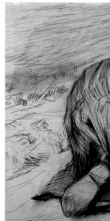

■ *The Old Cemetery Tower at Neunen*, May 1885, Van Gogh Museum, Amsterdam. Vincent painted this picture just before the

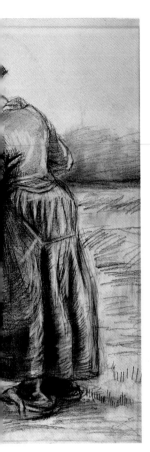

■ *Peasant Woman Raking*, August 1885, Kröller-Müller Museum, Otterlo. The figures in this series resemble those by Millet, but they are more solemn and real. Vincent wrote that he felt painting peasants at work was "truly modern". He thought about it every day.

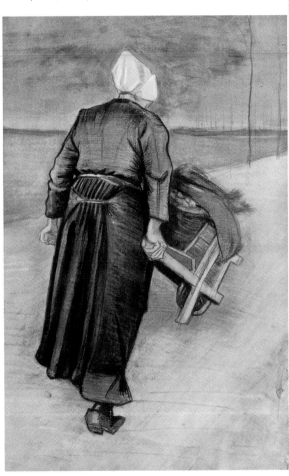

tower was demolished. Circling above the tower is a flock of black ravens, almost an obsessive metaphor of the artist's fate.

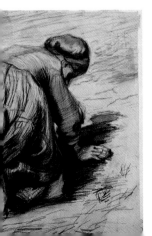

■ *Peasant Woman Kneeling*, Summer 1885, Nasjonalgalleriet, Oslo. Often executed as lithographs, Vincent van Gogh's drawings were probably preparatory sketches for paintings that sometimes never became reality.

■ *Peasant Woman with a Wheelbarrow*, 1883, Private Collection. The work of female peasants is portrayed with moving touches. Vincent thought that women were closer to nature, and, as a consequence, to sacredness.

BACKGROUND

# Millet and "The Angelus"

■ Jean-François Millet, *Woman Feeding her Child*, July 1888, Musée des Beaux-Arts, Marseille. Inspired by Christian portrayals of the Madonna, this work illustrates an ideal of maternal tenderness.

■ *The Woodcutter*, 1885, Frans Hals Museum, Haarlem. Praising Millet's *The Sower*, Gauthier wrote: "That man seemed to be made out of the earth he was working". Van Gogh considered Millet, rather than Manet, "to be that essentially modern painter who opened a new horizon to many".

"I do see the majestic beauty of a sunset, but, on the misty plains, I also see a man whose horses have been crying all day. He is bending over, and trying to lift his head for a brief moment of respite. His drama is enveloped in the splendor of nature. The expression 'the scream from the earth' is not something I discovered, but a truth that comes from the past." Thus wrote Jean-François Millet, a painter whom van Gogh greatly admired in his first years as an artist. Millet was born in Gréville in 1814. Driven by the need to move from an art based on Classical models, he abandoned the studio of historical painter Paul Delaroche to join the Barbizon School, which promoted a closer rapport with the natural world. Millet's melancholic scenes of peasant life and labor are the ideal visualization of the concepts expressed by the historian Jules Michelet: "Peasants do not merely constitute the largest part of the nation. They also represent the strongest, healthiest, and – upon careful examination of all factors, both physical and moral – best part of the nation".

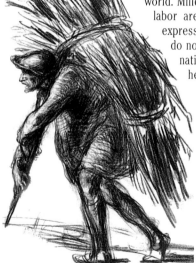

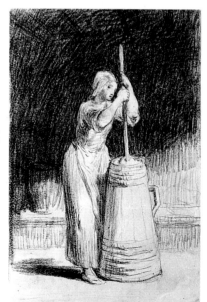

■ *Woman Churning Milk*, 1885, Szépmüvészeti Múzeum, Budapest. Inspired by Millet, van Gogh invested many of his characters an aura of holiness and pastoral eternity. As Millet before him, he turned even the most simple daily routine into a sacred, noble deed.

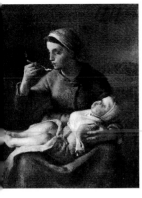

■ Jean-François Millet,
*The Angelus*, 1857–59,
Musée d'Orsay, Paris.
In an attempt to convey
his enthusiasm for Millet
to his brother Theo,
Vincent wrote, "that
picture by Millet,
*The Angelus*, that is
beauty, that is poetry".

■ Jean-François Millet,
*The Gleaners*, 1857,
Musée d'Orsay, Paris.
These women have a
monumental weight
that is reminiscent of
the biblical episode
of Ruth and Naomi in
the field of Boaz. In this
painting, Millet transcends
the everyday reality of
the peasants' life, imbuing
the scene with a strong
sense of dignity.

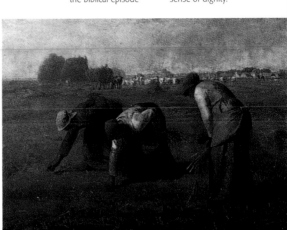

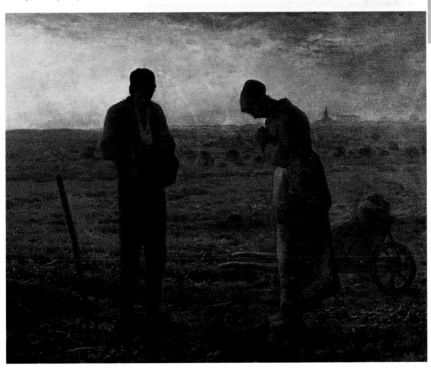

# Peasant Woman

Vincent often sketched faces in order to render them realistically in his paintings. This portrait, created in 1885 and now in the Van Gogh Museum, Amsterdam, shows Gordina de Groot, who also appears on the left-hand side of *The Potato Eaters*.

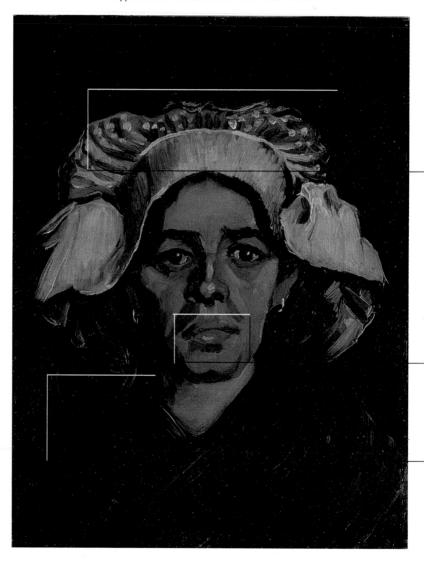

■ Frans Hals, *Regents of the St. Elizabeth Hospital of Haarlem*, 1641, Frans Hals Museum, Haarlem. Along with Rembrandt, Hals was the master of 17th-century Flemish art that most influenced van Gogh. In particular, Vincent admired the expressive way in which the Haarlem painter used the color black.

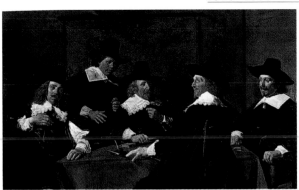

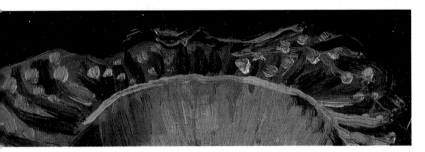

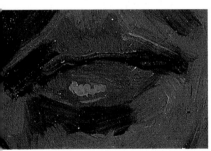

■ The girl's mouth is realized with quick strokes of color applied with a spatula. A touch of light highlights the frontal position and the genuineness and rigor of the young woman who braves her human condition with dignity.

■ Gordina de Groot's portrait is mostly painted with a variety of brown shades and the dull tone of the headgear is suited to these hues. Although the bonnet is painted in a beige color, the overall effect of the picture enables it to come across as white.

■ A real technical *tour de force*, the girl's shoulder is painted black on a black background. Van Gogh wrote that these figures were infinitely beautiful, "but no subjects in painting are as difficult as these".

With Rembrandt-like intensity, the girl's face emerges from the darkness of the picture, and shines of a light that seems to come from the soul.

# The portrayal of work

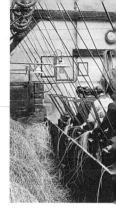

Since the Middle Ages, the labors of the seasons had been a theme in painting and illumination: rural workers appeared in calendars and were sometimes included in the iconography of the Nativity. However, peasants were usually portrayed as the level between man and beast, possessing common sense but unable to lead an intellectual life. In the 16th century, they took center stage in the work of several artists, such as Bruegel and Le Nain. Pieter Bruegel the Elder (c.1525–69) was the first painter to portray the reality of their world: he described the peasants' customs without any idealization or grotesque parody. In the 1800s, artists often inserted figures of shepherds and peasants in idyllic landscapes that had no connection with the real world: one of the first painters to go against this trend and portray the harshness and the necessity of physical work was Gustave Courbet. In 1830s France, George Sand's novels contributed to changing the way in which the working community was perceived and, after the 1848 Revolution, the working man became the main character in Realist art, since he combined an eternal myth with everyday reality.

■ While the first portrayals of work focused on the toil of farmers, in the 1900s artists were forced to face the increasingly problematic question of the urban proletariat.

■ Gustave Courbet, *The Stonebreakers*, 1849, formerly in the Gemäldegalerie, Dresden, but destroyed during World War II. Shown at the Salon of 1851, Courbet's work aroused a scandal.

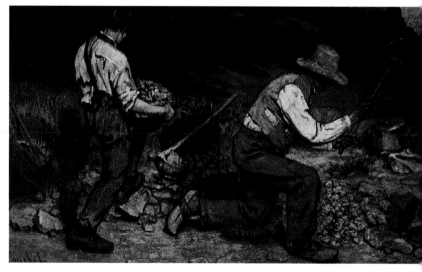

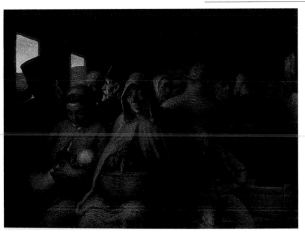

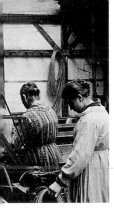

■ Honoré Daumier, *The Third-Class Carriage*, c.1862, National Gallery of Canada, Ottawa. In his works, Daumier used a haunting style to portray human suffering. His art conveys his own feelings of excitement in front of the changes of his time. Compared by Balzac to Michelangelo, Daumier strove to render in his works every aspect of the "human comedy".

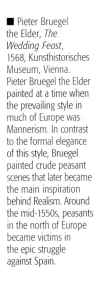

■ Pieter Bruegel the Elder, *The Wedding Feast*, 1568, Kunsthistorisches Museum, Vienna. Pieter Bruegel the Elder painted at a time when the prevailing style in much of Europe was Mannerism. In contrast to the formal elegance of this style, Bruegel painted crude peasant scenes that later became the main inspiration behind Realism. Around the mid-1550s, peasants in the north of Europe became victims in the epic struggle against Spain.

## Pieter Bruegel the Elder

Little is known about the life and career of this Netherlandish master. Karel van Mander's biography, published in 1604, tells us that he joined the painter's guild in Antwerp in 1551. After a long journey to Italy in about 1553, he developed an almost monumental tone in his painting. The subjects of his most famous works are not characters from the upper classes, but peasants and farmers. Bruegel portrayed some of the most compassionate scenes of village life, for example in *The Massacre of the Innocents*. He initiated a new iconographic style in western art, which found a literary equivalent in the picaresque novel. In direct opposition to the intellectualism of the Renaissance, Bruegel's peasants are the first example of pictorial realism.

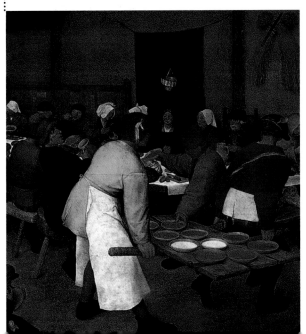

MASTERPIECES

# The Potato Eaters

Executed in April 1885 and kept at the Van Gogh Museum in Amsterdam, this painting was conceived as a summation of Vincent's artistic studies. It conveys his social feelings with great strength and intensity.

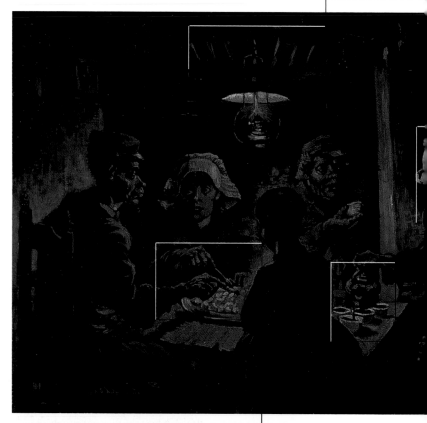

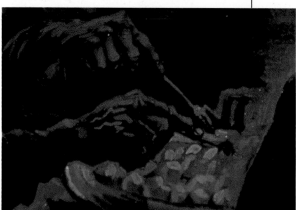

■ The peasants' hands are rendered with pathetic simplicity: they have the same color and consistency as the very potatoes that they have dug. The apparently random brushstrokes are in fact precisely and sparingly used.

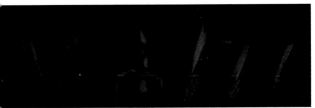

■ Within the darkness of the room, the lamp and the barely visible rafters increase the sense of solemnity. The viewer is reminded of the darkness of a cathedral.

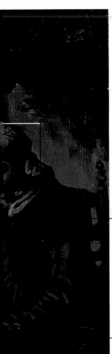

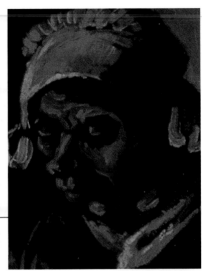

■ The female peasant's face is impressively rendered with a sparing use of half tones. In the background, lighter, thinner strokes help to bring the figure into profile against the shade. The uncompromising portrayal of these characters indicates Vincent's desire to create "a real *peasant picture*…painting them in their roughness [rather] than giving them a conventional charm".

■ Van Gogh is the ideal painter of peasant life: he felt a great solidarity with poor people, whose lives, like his own, were full of suffering. The table becomes an altar, and food the sacrament shared by the farmers. The act of distributing food and drink further underlines the theme of a spiritual communion. The light on the objects in this room is similar to the light Vincent had seen in the mines, while the darkness has a physical thickness.

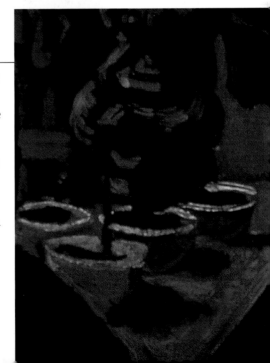

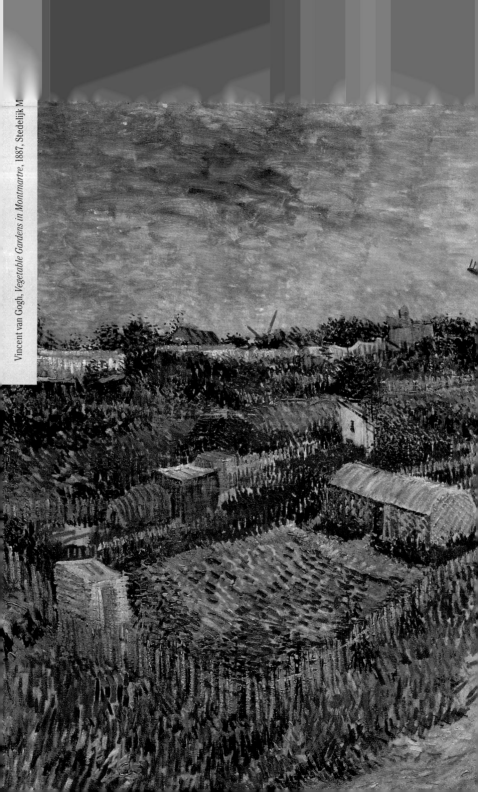

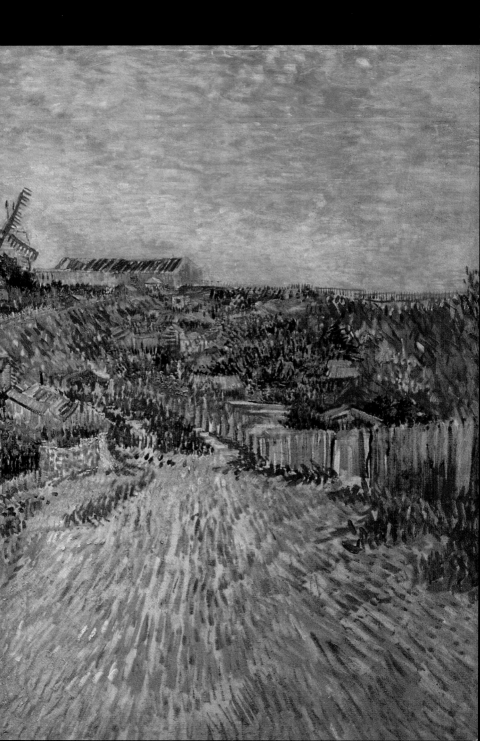

# From sadness to joy

After his father's death Vincent grew closer to his brother, and joined him in Paris, where he lived from March 1886 until February 1888. Theo lived in a flat in rue de Laval, known today as rue Victor Massé, near Pigalle. To Vincent, he represented family but also his key to the Parisian art world. Van Gogh immediately enrolled at the famous studio of Fernand Cormon, where he became friendly with other students, such as Henri de Toulouse-Lautrec and the Australian John Russell, who later became a friend of Claude Monet and Auguste Rodin, and whose advice inspired Henri Matisse. After a few months, the two brothers moved to 54 rue Lepic, near Montmartre. Vincent's ambition was to create a new artistic group with his painter friends and, encouraged by Theo, he wrote that there would be more color in his paintings and more enthusiasm in his life. Vincent saw color in a new way: the powerful light he had admired in the art of Rembrandt and Tintoretto turned into the delicate tonal gradations that characterize his Parisian landscapes. He enjoyed the international atmosphere of Paris: the city attracted artists from all over the world, such as Max Liebermann from Germany, James Abbott McNeil Whistler and Mary Cassatt from the United States, and Felicien Rops from Belgium.

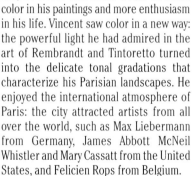

■ Victor Hugo's funeral rites, portrayed here in a contemporary photograph, had taken place in Paris on May 30, 1885, some months before Vincent's arrival.

■ *La Guinguette a Montmartre*, October 1886, Musée d'Orsay, Paris. In 1887 Vincent wrote to his sister telling her that, after living for so many years with no desire to smile, he now felt the need to burst out laughing.

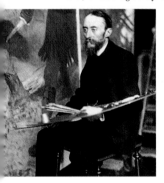

■ Portrayed here at work, Fernand Cormon opened his own studio at 104 Avenue de Clichy following his triumph at the 1880 Salon. His teachings, based on copying works initially, and painting from life at a later stage, discouraged Vincent, who said he did not find Cormon as useful as he expected.

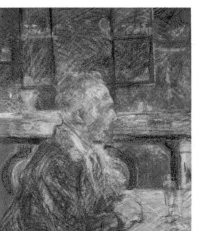

■ Henri de Toulouse-Lautrec, *Portrait of van Gogh*, 1887, Van Gogh Museum, Amsterdam. Although very different, the two artists had great admiration and respect for each other. In 1890, Toulouse-Lautrec challenged De Groux to a duel for refusing to show his own works next to van Gogh's "abominable" art.

### Victor Hugo (1802–85)

Along with Dickens, Hugo was one of the first great authors of popular literature. Characters from *Les Misérables* and *Toilers of the Sea* were readily adopted as working-class heroes by the public. Their honesty redeemed them from their misery. Hugo's books were passed from one generation to another. When his bier was carried to the Pantheon, Maurice Barrès commented that the whole of humanity had gathered around a great man.

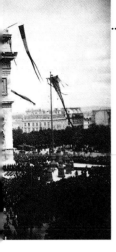

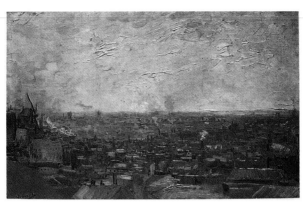

■ *View of Paris from Montmartre*, 1886, Kunstmuseum, Basel. This is one of several cityscapes that Vincent made shortly after his arrival in Paris.

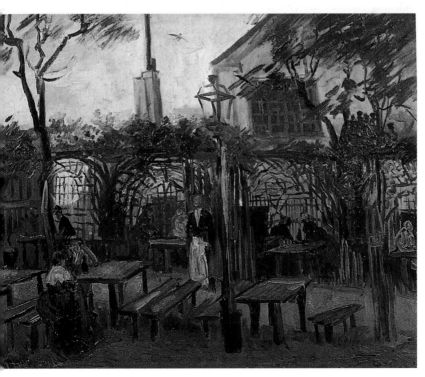

# From Impressionism to Symbolism

■ Portrayed below is Joris-Karl Huysmans (1847–1907). He rejected the pragmatism sweeping the nation and, in his novel *À rebours* (1884), created the character of Des Esseintes, a refined aesthete who collects Redon's drawings.

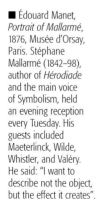

When van Gogh arrived in Paris, the Impressionist movement that had animated the Parisian art scene in the 1870s was beginning to dissolve. In opposition to the representational worlds of Realism and Impressionism, another movement, inspired by the most mysterious and spiritual traits of Romanticism, briefly flourished. It was part of a broad anti-rationalist trend in philosophy, literature, and art towards the end of the century. French poets such as Paul Verlaine, Arthur Rimbaud, and Stéphane Mallarmé proposed a nonmaterialistic reading of reality, resurrecting medieval views of art as an alchemy of hidden meanings. The literary movement found its visual equivalent in the works of Gustave Moreau and Odilon Redon, who gave visual expression to their emotional experiences in paintings and drawings. The poet Jean Moréas defined the Symbolist aim in the movement's manifesto, published in *Le Figaro* in 1886: "to clothe the idea in sensuous form". Although impressed by the strong mystical traits of Symbolism, van Gogh remained indifferent to the excessive aestheticism promoted by some artists in the trend.

■ Édouard Manet, *Portrait of Mallarmé*, 1876, Musée d'Orsay, Paris. Stéphane Mallarmé (1842–98), author of *Hérodiade* and the main voice of Symbolism, held an evening reception every Tuesday. His guests included Maeterlinck, Wilde, Whistler, and Valéry. He said: "I want to describe not the object, but the effect it creates".

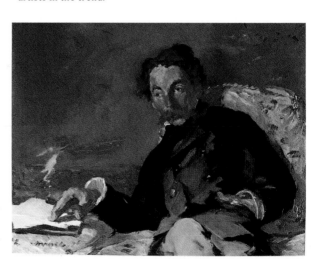

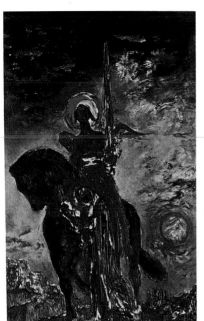

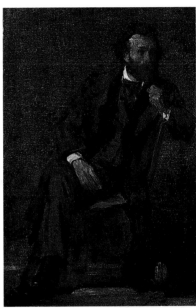

■ Gustave Moreau, *The Parca and the Angel of Death*, 1890, Musée Gustave Moreau, Paris. Rejecting the realism inherent in Impressionism, Moreau preferred mystical imagery, evoking lost civilizations and mythologies in his strange paintings.

■ Edgar Degas, *Portrait of Gustave Moreau*, c.1860, Musée Gustave Moreau, Paris. A refined lover of Persian, Hindu and Byzantine art, Moreau communicated his enthusiasm for painting to famous students such as Matisse, Marquet, and Rouault.

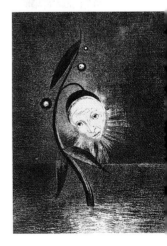

■ Odilon Redon, *The Marsh Flower*, 1885, Bibliothèque Nationale, Paris. Inspired by the stories by Edgar Allan Poe, Redon epitomized the fantastical elements of Symbolism.

■ Odilon Redon, *The Chariot of Apollo*, detail, 1910–11, Abbey Library, Fontfroide. "My drawings", claimed Redon, "have the same place as music within the world of the indeterminate".

**1886–1887**

# Le Tambourin

This painting, executed in 1887, portrays Agostina Segatori in the Tambourin, one of the lively cabaret-cafés in Montmartre frequented by Vincent and his circle of artist friends.

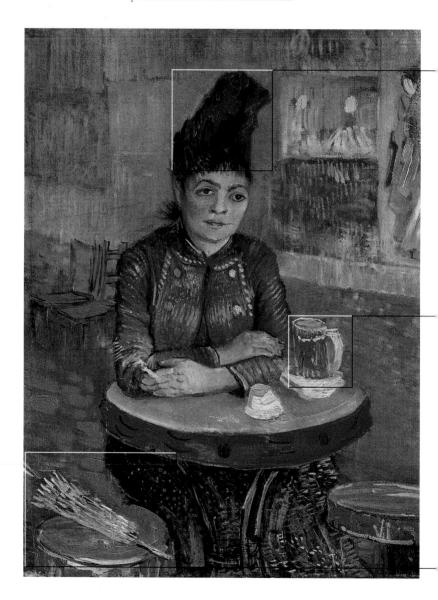

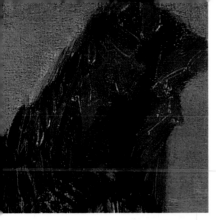

■ Vincent wanted to reproduce the different effects created by surrounding light on colors. The interior of the Tambourin has a wan light, and the main dull colors are brought to life by the red of the table and the unusual hat.

■ Edgar Degas, L'Absinthe, 1876, Musée d'Orsay, Paris. With this painting, Degas created one of the most disturbing images of the solitude and moral degradation suffered by people living in large cities.

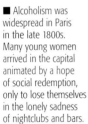

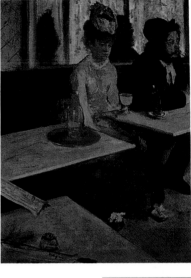

■ Alcoholism was widespread in Paris in the late 1800s. Many young women arrived in the capital animated by a hope of social redemption, only to lose themselves in the lonely sadness of nightclubs and bars.

■ Vincent used rapid strokes of blue and white to render the delicate folds of the parasol.

■ Édouard Manet, The Plum, 1877, National Gallery of Art, Washington. In this evocative work, Manet portrays a disillusioned girl alone in a café at night. Her untouched glass and unlit cigarette indicate her poverty.

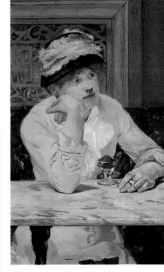

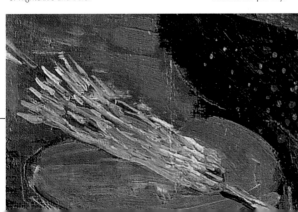

# A good painter and a kind man: Pissarro

"**A** humble, colossal master": thus did Paul Cézanne define Pissarro, who worked with him for some time in the countryside around Pontoise. Camille Pissarro was born in the Lesser Antilles in 1830 from a family of Jewish faith. He arrived in Paris in 1855 and took part in all the Impressionist exhibitions. With his affectionate ways, he tried to keep together the group of his artist friends, which was often undermined by personal and ideological differences. Although he often had financial problems himself, Pissarro always tried his best to help young struggling artists. He took in Paul Gauguin upon the latter's return from Martinique, and understood the feelings of restlessness plaguing Vincent van Gogh, with whom he shared a sense of warmth towards simple folk. When Vincent organized a show of Impressionist works with Theo, he asked Pissarro for some paintings to exhibit next to his own, and it was with him and his son Lucien that, before moving to Arles, van Gogh discussed a project for an independent body of artists and merchants. In later years, Vincent kept on asking Theo about the comments Pissarro had expressed on his works.

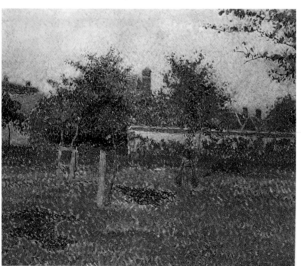

■ Camille Pissarro, *Woman in a Meadow, Spring, Eragny-sur-Epte*, 1888, Musée d'Orsay, Paris. A fierce Republican, during the Franco-Prussian War, Pissarro and his family had to move to England. Upon his return to France, he found that a large part of the house at Pontoise had been burnt and many of his works destroyed. However, he started painting again, confident in his art and in the social role of beauty.

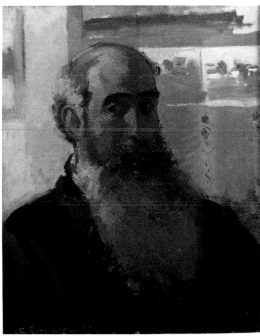

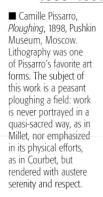

■ Camille Pissarro, *Ploughing*, 1898, Pushkin Museum, Moscow. Lithography was one of Pissarro's favorite art forms. The subject of this work is a peasant ploughing a field: work is never portrayed in a quasi-sacred way, as in Millet, nor emphasized in its physical efforts, as in Courbet, but rendered with austere serenity and respect.

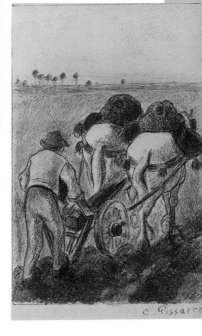

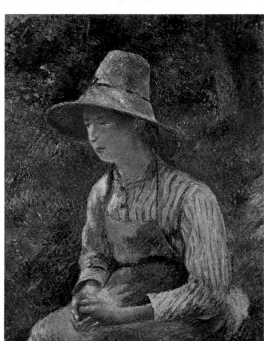

■ Camille Pissarro, *Peasant Girl with a Straw Hat*, 1881, National Gallery of Art, Washington. This young peasant girl has nothing in common with Manet's elegant figures. Still and meditative, she wholly belongs to the natural environment.

47

**1886–1887**

# Montmartre

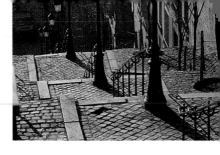

Following rue Lepic, a long street leading from rue des Abbesses to the Moulin de la Galette, Vincent could reach the quarter of Montmartre within minutes. He painted the area's tiny gardens, the drinking places, and the Moulin de la Galette, which he portrayed from various points of view. Later on, when searching for new subjects, he moved to the outskirts of the city. He used to travel for several kilometers, venturing as far as Asnières, Joinville, Suresnes, and Château. Following Seurat's example, he became a regular on the Île de la Grande Jatte. But it was Montmartre that held his heart, not least for the presence there of the simple people that he so tenderly portrayed in his works. Around him, the city quivered with the excitement of new artistic expressions, such as Arthur Rimbaud's *Illuminations*, Émile Zola's *L'Oeuvre*, and Wagner's *Lohengrin*. Among the colorful characters of Montmartre, Vincent met Suzanne Valadon, painter and model, also known as the "terrible Suzanne", as Edgar Degas called her.

■ The steps towards Place du Tertre are one of the most famous walks in the world. Van Gogh painted his Parisian roofs from here.

■ *Le Moulin de la Galette*, 1886, Nationalgalerie, Berlin. This version was painted in October 1886. Vincent used to visit this establishment with fellow artist Toulouse-Lautrec.

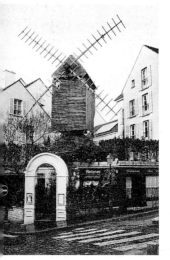

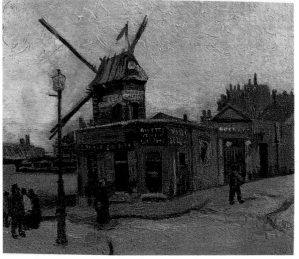

■ The Radet mill, in the photo above, was in Rue Girardon, in the heart of Montmartre and only a short walk from the van Gogh residence.

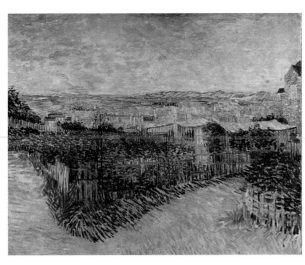

■ *Vegetable Gardens in Montmartre*, 1887, Van Gogh Museum, Amsterdam. Throughout 1886, Montmartre maintained a rustic character that Vincent liked. He wrote that French air clears the head and does one good.

■ *Le Moulin de la Galette*, 1886, Carnegie Institute, Pittsburgh. Vincent often wandered around the fields where Renoir's children played. He was looking for new angles from which to portray the Parisian quarter of Montmartre. This area reminded him of a rustic village in Île de France.

■ Le Cafè de la Nouvelle-Athènes in Place Pigalle replaced the Cafè Guerbois as a meeting place for artists. It was here that Degas painted *L'Absinthe* and that the Impressionists found their first supporters.

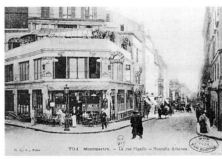

■ At the time, the Moulin de la Galette was an open-air dance hall that owed its name to the pancakes (*galettes*) that were served there. Renoir left a lasting impression of Sunday dances at the Moulin in his famous painting of the subject.

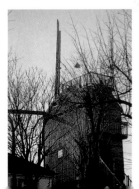

**1886–1887**

# Portrait of Père Tanguy

Père Tanguy, a committed follower of the Impressionists and the Parisian avant-garde, sold artist's materials and would often accept paintings in lieu of payment. Painted in 1887, this portrait is now part of a private collection.

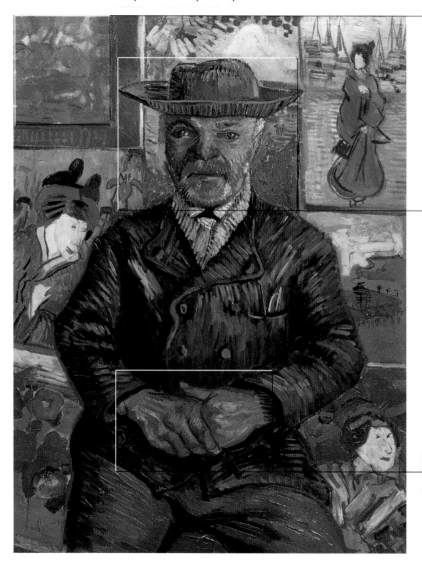

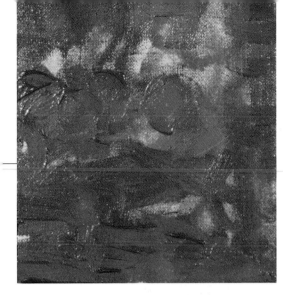

■ The idea of surrounding sitters with objects that reflect their life and interests was not a new one. Other examples are provided by the portrait of Zola by Manet, and the one of Tissot by Degas. By portraying Tanguy against a background of Japanese prints, van Gogh demonstrates both his deep affection for the man, and their shared passion for eastern art.

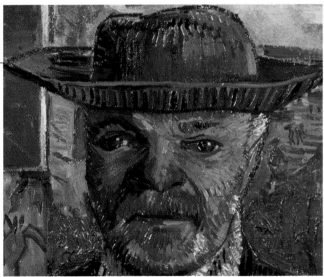

■ Vincent seems to carry out a research of Tanguy's best qualities. The rough features of the sitter, especially his eyes, are rendered with intensity: his face is lively, and his spirit comes across in both his expression and the brushstrokes.

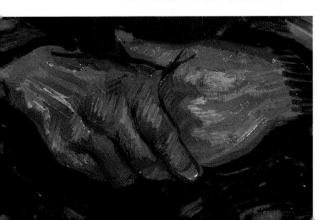

■ Tanguy's frontal pose is reminiscent of both medieval art and early photography. The figure and the background are unified by color: the dominant reds and greens of the prints are echoed in the hands and face.

51

**1886-1887**

# The Japanese influence

■ *Bridge in the Rain*, October 1887, Van Gogh Museum, Amsterdam. This painting is a copy of a woodcut by Ando Hiroshige, one of the many Japanese prints in Vincent's collection.

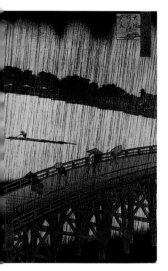

In 1853 Japan made its entrance in the international markets: Europe enthusiastically discovered Japanese art objects and paintings, which were immediately exported and shown at the Universal Exhibition in Paris. The term *Japonism* was coined by critic Philippe Burty who used it to indicate a wide range of western interpretations of Japanese art: from a simple adaptation of eastern decorative motifs, to the analysis and integration of the principles of oriental art. Many artists were inspired by the new wave: Claude Monet decorated the walls of his flat with Japanese prints, Édouard Manet was inspired to use flat areas of color in his own paintings, and Henry Rivière engraved *Thirty-six Views of the Eiffel Tower* in homage to Katsushika Hokusai. Van Gogh adopted the philosophy of oriental art, especially the subtle yet reverential observation of nature, and even claimed that the south of France was the European equivalent of Japan. He mused on whether these artists taught "some kind of religion", noting how they lived within nature as if they were flowers themselves. Vincent bought many Japanese prints, especially from the famous art dealer Samuel Bing, editor of the magazine *Le Japon illustré* and curator of an exhibition of oriental works of art in the Café Le Tambourin.

■ Ando Hiroshige, *Evening Squall on Great Bridge in Atake*, c.1857, Österreichisches Museum für angewandte Kunst, Vienna.

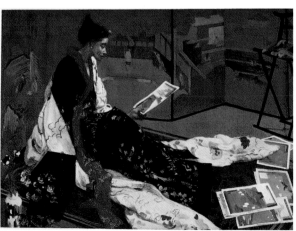

■ James Abbott McNeil Whistler, *Caprice in Purple and Gold, No. 2*, 1864, Freer Gallery of Art, Washington. Whistler was one of the first artists to incorporate oriental influences into his work.

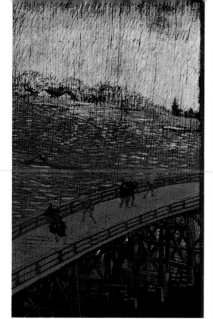

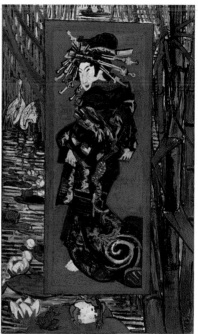

■ *Japonaiserie: Oiran* (after Keisai Eisen), July–September 1887, Van Gogh Museum, Amsterdam. The print by Eisen that Vincent copied for this work had appeared on the cover of a Japan issue of *Paris Illustré*, a magazine published by Theo's company. Vincent was especially interested in the diagonal setting of some prints, which was used to underline the dynamism of the scene.

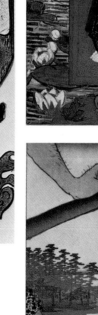

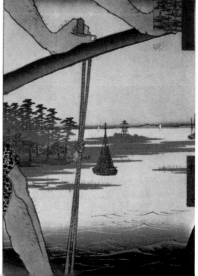

■ Henri de Toulouse-Lautrec, *Jean Avril*, c.1896, Bibliothèque Nationale, Paris. The flat, bold colors and cropped design are devices taken from Japanese prints.

■ Andô Hiroshige, *Temple of the Prey*, c.1858, Museum für ostasiatische Kunst, Cologne. From the Japanese, van Gogh learned to adopt unusual viewpoints.

**1886–1887**

# Self-Portrait with the Easel

In this self-portrait, one of a series executed while in Paris, Vincent explores his identity much as Rembrandt had done. The steady, powerful presentation is indebted to Cézanne. It is now in the Van Gogh Museum, Amsterdam.

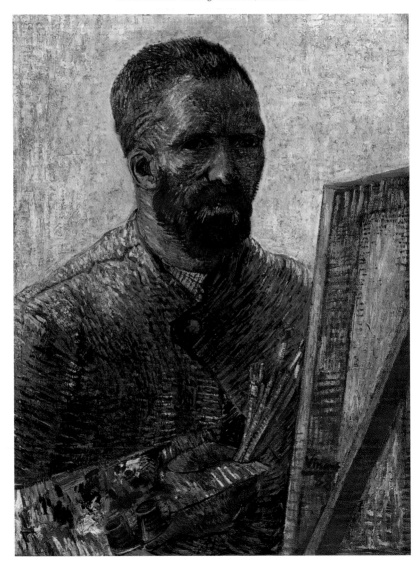

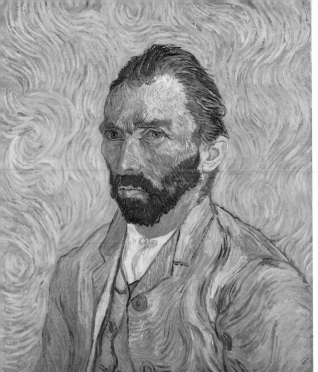

■ *Self-Portrait*,
September 1889,
Musée d'Orsay, Paris.
Van Gogh's self-portraits
enable the observer
to trace the tragic curve
of his life. Painted
only a year after his
*Self-Portrait with the
Easel*, this painting
was executed during
Vincent's hospitalization
in Saint-Rémy. One
can almost sense the
struggle of the artist
to control his choleric,
passionate temperament.

■ *Self-Portrait with
Palette*, August 1889,
Whitney Collection,
New York. The palette
comes across as a
defence barrier, almost
a shield in Vincent's
battle against evil.
The blue background
seems shaken by a
great energy, and it
testifies to the artist's
restlessness, but also
to his mental strength.
From the dark center
of the deep blue, van
Gogh's head emerges
with brilliant intensity:
his beard and hair
are rendered with
the same color of the
moon in *Starry Night*
(pp. 106–107).

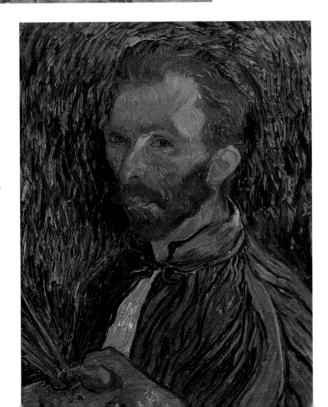

55

**1886–1887**

# Vincent and the Impressionists

The crisis of the Impressionist movement started in earnest in 1886, the year in which Vincent van Gogh arrived in Paris. Even the ever faithful Pissarro temporarily abandoned the immediate, spontaneous art typical of the Impressionists to experiment with the divisionist techniques of the Neo-Impressionists. The eighth Impressionist exhibition introduced many new artists, such as Georges Seurat, Paul Gauguin, Jean-Louis Forain, and Federico Zandomeneghi. Claude Monet, now living in Giverny, was moving towards the symbolism of his last water-lily paintings, while Renoir rediscovered Raphael's art after travelling to Italy. It was time to consider new horizons. Van Gogh commented that Impressionist art was brilliant, but a little superficial and not completely rewarding. During his time in Paris, Vincent discovered the works of Adolphe Monticelli, an artist who had lived as a romantic *bohémien*, and who had died in Marseille on June 29, 1886, in a solitude tinged by insanity. Vincent wrote that he sometimes felt that Monticelli's life went on within him.

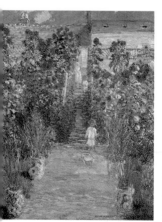

■ Claude Monet, *The Artist's Garden at Vétheuil*, 1880, National Gallery of Art, Washington. Monet encouraged observers of his art to reject academic formalism and focus on the importance of perception. His quick brushstrokes deftly demonstrate the interaction of colors.

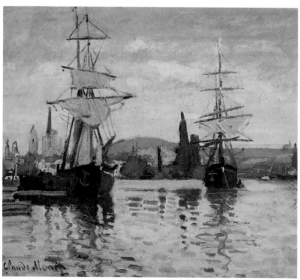

■ Claude Monet, *Ships on the Seine*, 1880, National Gallery of Art, Washington.

■ Theo van Gogh was four years younger than Vincent. Like him, he had a good eye for painting.

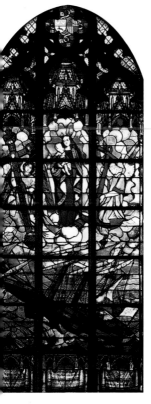

■ The window of the Maris Stella Andrieskerk in Antwerp was created in the 1500s. Van Gogh combined his knowledge of Impressionist art with a passion for the shining colors used in stained-glass windows. Vincent was particularly fond of this window in Antwerp, not least because of the subject: Mary helping a ship in danger.

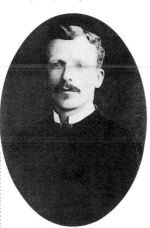

## Theo van Gogh

Vincent was introduced to the Impressionists by his brother Theo (1857–91), who worked in Paris for the Boussod and Valadon gallery. He became Vincent's "double", as proven by the hundreds of letters the painter sent him, allowing him to take part in his every mood or thought. Although aware of the disapproval of his family, Theo sent money to Vincent as often as he could. A few months after his brother's death, Theo fell ill: he died on January 25, 1891. Although his letters are less demonstrative, he wrote of the deep sorrow he felt whenever he thought of Vincent's death.

■ *Memory of the Garden in Etten,* sketch sent to Wilhelmine, 1888. More than 800 letters survive from Vincent's collection, and they provide an insightful analysis of his works. Often, as in this case, words and sketches became one, as in an oriental scroll.

■ The van Goghs longed to be like the van Eyck brothers, the great Flemish artists of the 1500s. Vincent told Theo not to be surprised if he wrote often, since the thought of him was always in his soul.

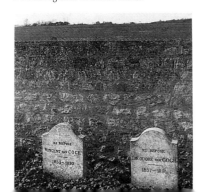

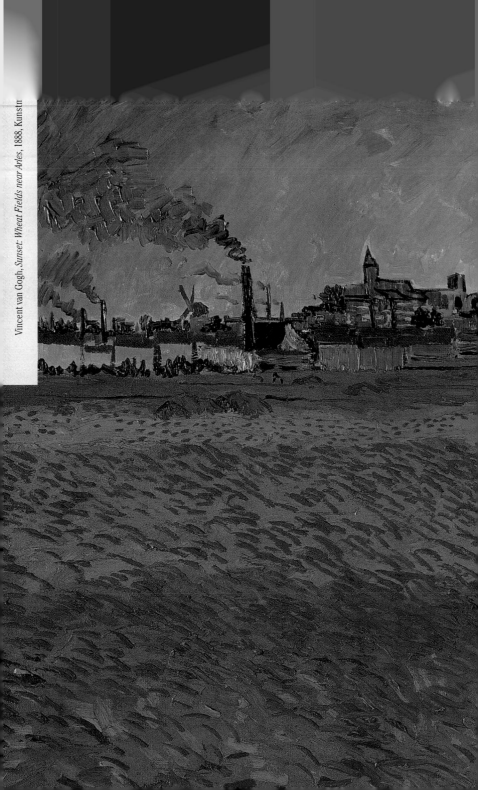

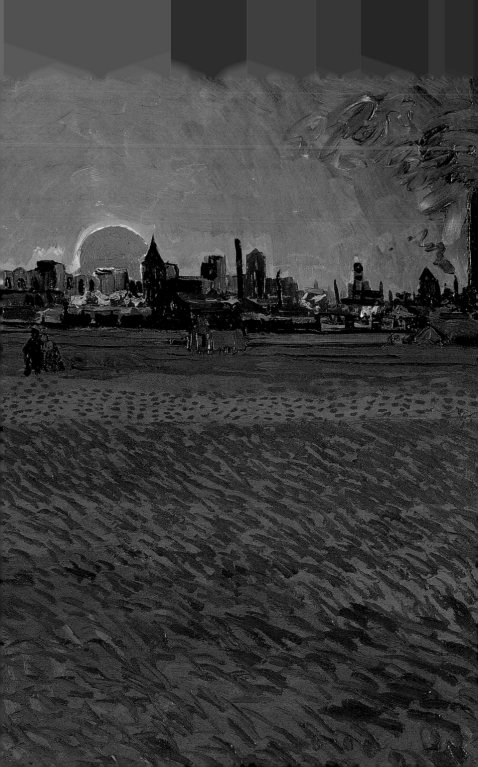

# In search of the sun

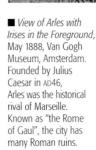

Looking for a place to retire and recover his peace of mind and self-confidence – without which, he felt, one inevitably withers – Vincent left Paris, its alcohol-fuelled nights, women, and exhausting crowds, and headed south. His plan was to reach Marseille, the city where painter Adolphe Monticelli, for whom Vincent had developed great respect and admiration, had died. In the end, he settled in Arles, in Provence. The Japanese prints that van Gogh had amassed affected his idea of the Midi. In March 1888, he wrote to Émile Bernard, claiming that the south of France resembled Japan: the air was clear, the colors bright, and the watercourses across the fields were emerald green or deep blue just like in the prints. Arriving in Arles in February 1888, he wrote that in the south the senses became more acute, the hand quicker, the eye livelier, and the mind clearer. He stayed at the Hotel Carrell, in 30 rue Cavalerie, and eventually rented a house in 2 place Lamartine, just above the Café de la Gare, owned by Joseph and Marie Ginoux. This was the famous "Yellow House" where van Gogh hoped to create a community of artists along the lines of the brotherhood of Dutch painters in the 17th century. Vincent survived on little money and was reliant on Theo's contribution.

■ *View of Arles with Irises in the Foreground,* May 1888, Van Gogh Museum, Amsterdam. Founded by Julius Caesar in AD46, Arles was the historical rival of Marseille. Known as "the Rome of Gaul", the city has many Roman ruins.

■ Montmajour Abbey lies only 5 kilometers (3 miles) northeast of Arles. Founded in the 6th century, the abbey looks from a rocky promontory onto the plain of La Crau. The sides of the headland are rich in cytisus, a winter plant that might have been introduced in France by the Saracens.

■ This is a view of Saint-Rémy. Just north of Arles, Saint-Rémy was one of Vincent's favorite walking destinations.

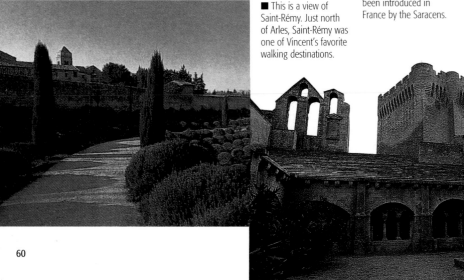

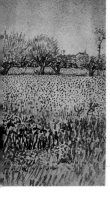

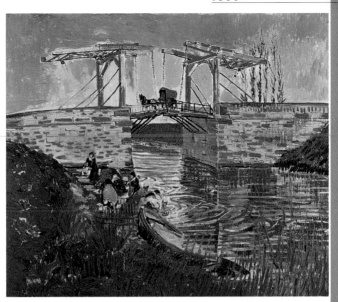

■ *The Langlois Bridge at Arles*, 1888, Kröller-Müller Museum, Otterlo. Usually called Langlois Bridge from the name of an old keeper, this bridge is no longer in existence. However, the local tourist industry has funded the rebuilding of a rough model.

■ *The Langlois Bridge at Arles*, 1888, Private Collection, Paris. In this canvas, executed in April 1888, a month after the Otterlo version, Vincent replaces the delicate touches with a more intense chromaticism.

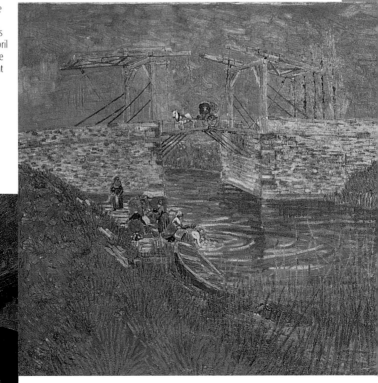

**1888**

# The Pink Orchard

"I'm up to my ears in work, for the trees are in blossom and I want to paint a Provençal orchard of astounding gaiety." In spring 1888, Vincent created a series of orchard paintings. This work is in the Van Gogh Museum in Amsterdam.

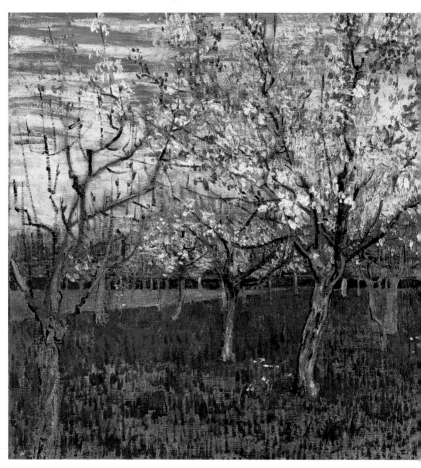

■ *The White Orchard*, April 1888, Van Gogh Museum, Amsterdam. This painting is Vincent's aesthetic response to the clear light in the south. In a letter to Bernard, he explained his technique, which

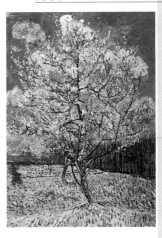

■ *Blossoming Pear Tree*, April 1888, Van Gogh Museum, Amsterdam. This is truly a *haiku*, a Japanese poem on the brief, delicate beauty of this thin tree that turns all its strength into blossoms.

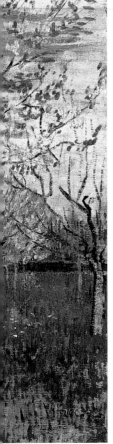

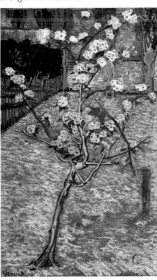

■ *Peach Trees in Blossom*, April–May 1888, Van Gogh Museum, Amsterdam. Vincent's paintings of trees in blossom confirm the influence of Japanese prints on his work. For this work, he has chosen a low vantage point, silhouetting the branches against the blue sky.

involved blending the colors, leaving some areas of the canvas untouched and some to be completed. Van Gogh was especially delighted with the sky, painted as a frenetic mixture of glorious white and blue.

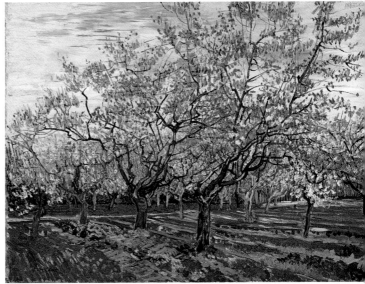

**1888**

# The charm of
# an ancient city

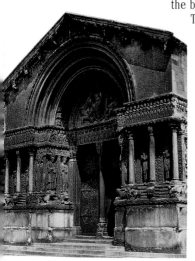

Les Alyscamps in Arles is a pagan graveyard where, according to legend, Christ himself appeared to the first bishop of the city as he was about to consecrate it. For centuries Celts and Romans buried their relatives there, in the belief that it was the best way towards the Elysian Fields. The cemetery was used throughout the Middle Ages. Another important monument, and a marvellous example of the Provençal Romanesque style, is the façade of Saint-Trophime, which dates back to the 12th century, and in structure is reminiscent of a Roman triumphal arch. Although today the splendid church attracts many tourists, when van Gogh was in Arles it was neglected and covered in moss. Vincent wrote that the portal fascinated him: he found it admirable and monstrous at the same time, "like a Chinese nightmare", and he felt that this great monument belonged to a different world. For Vincent, the city held another charm, the Arlesians (the people of Arles). He had certainly read the novel *Max Havelaar*, in which the author Multatuli mentioned that the women in Arles were possibly the most beautiful in the south of Europe, with dark eyes, jet black curls, and a regal posture.

■ Close to the ruins of the arena and the theatre, the splendid cathedral of Saint-Trophime looks onto the main town square. The portal is visibly of Classic derivation.

■ The cloister of Saint-Trophime is the most heavily decorated in Provence: the coupled columns that constitute it are adorned with elaborate capitals.

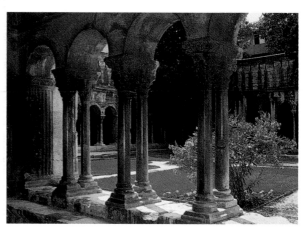

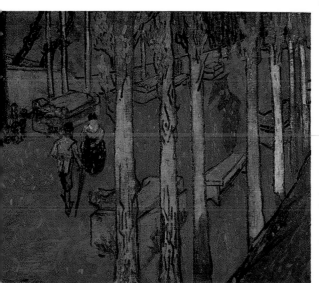

■ *Les Alyscamps*, November 1888, Kröller-Müller Museum, Otterlo. Although evidently influenced by Gauguin, the falling leaves in Vincent's painting place it within a distinct time frame. Gauguin's scene, on the contrary, is timeless.

■ Les Alyscamps, shown below, is traditionally associated with white magic. Beneath an avenue of poplars, sarcophagi from all over Europe have been placed alongside the "sacred way".

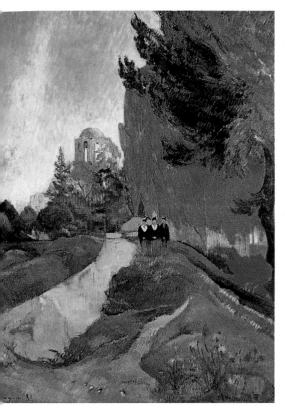

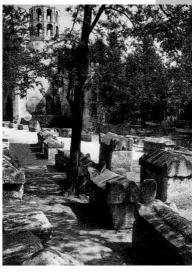

■ Paul Gauguin, *Les Alyscamps*, 1888, Musée d'Orsay, Paris. The ancient cemetery was the first subject painted by Vincent and Paul together. Here, three figures stand on the hill like the Fates, a recurring image in Gauguin's work.

**1888**

# Portrait of Eugène Boch

Vincent said that his sitter reminded him of a Flemish gentleman from the time of William the Silent, and that he would not be surprised if he was a kind man. The painting is housed at the Musée d'Orsay in Paris.

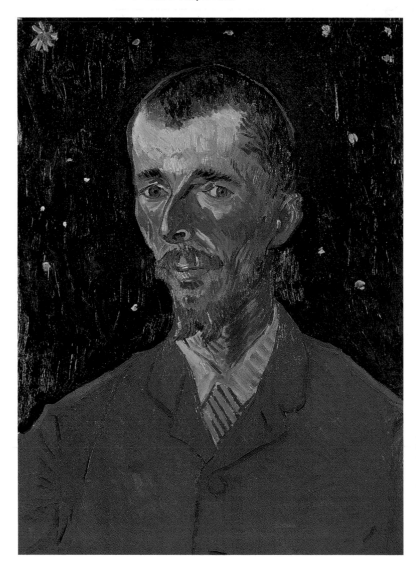

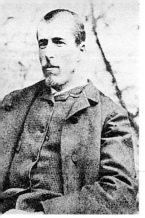

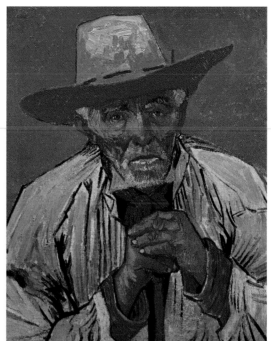

■ The son of a Belgian businessman transferred to Borinage, Boch arrived in Paris in 1879. In 1890, a few weeks before Vincent's death, Eugène's older sister Anna purchased one of his paintings, *The Red Vineyard*, which today is in the Pushkin Museum in Moscow.

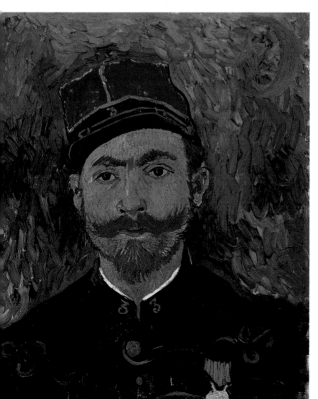

■ *Portrait of Patience Escalier*, 1888, Private Collection. Vincent wrote that this work, a portrait of a local peasant, portrays an innocent, sweet being in whose presence anything he learned in Paris became irrelevant.

■ *Portrait of Milliet*, September 1888, Kröller-Müller Museum, Otterlo. The star and moon crescent were the symbols of the Zouaves, while the medal was a reminder of Tonkin. Vincent's friendship with Milliet was brief: on November 1, 1888, the Second Lieutenant left to go to Algeria.

**1888**

# The Gauguin affair

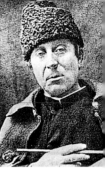

Van Gogh first met Gauguin in 1887 in Paris. In February 1888, Paul left the capital and moved to Pont-Aven in Brittany, where he worked with Émile Bernard and other artists. In the meantime, Vincent had moved to Arles: he followed the work of his colleagues and dreamed of gathering them in his "*Atelier du Midi*". His hopes became reality with Gauguin. The latter was plagued by financial problems, and Vincent persuaded him to agree to a cohabitation that would benefit both their art and their economic standing. Gauguin arrived in Arles at the end of October and remained at the "Yellow House" for only two months. The leader of the Pont-Aven School and founder of Synthetism, Gauguin assumed the role of mentor in Arles, and encouraged van Gogh to paint from the palette of his imagination. However, the Dutch artist preferred to paint from reality, in front of a model. The arguments between them became increasingly violent until, on December 23, 1888, van Gogh threatened Gauguin with a razor. In fear of his own life, Paul spent the night in a boarding house. The following morning the "Yellow House" was sieged by crowds and police: Vincent had cut off part of his left ear and presented it to a prostitute. Gauguin fled hurriedly.

■ After several years working as a stockbroker, Paul Gauguin (1848–1903) took his first steps in the art world under the guidance of Pissarro. From 1883, he dedicated his life to painting. He travelled to Tahiti in 1891 and moved there permanently in 1895.

■ Paul Gauguin, *Old Women at Arles*, 1888, The Art Institute of Chicago. This painting exemplifies the main difference between the two artists. Gauguin first observes the women and the setting, then portrays them not as they really are, but as they appear in his imagination, intentionally using unnatural colors.

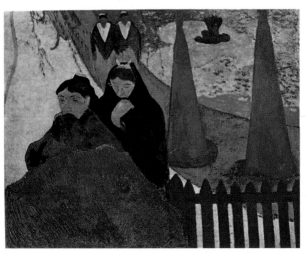

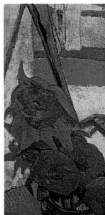

### The reasons for the conflict

The disastrous quarrel between the artists was due their different personalities and expectations. Vincent dreamed of an absolute friendship, a perfect fusion of intents and souls. Although Gauguin related to Vincent's torment, he was frightened by his temper, which could flare violently whenever he felt misunderstood. They also had different opinions on art. Van Gogh wrote that Gauguin fled like Napoleon leaving the army to fight in Egypt.

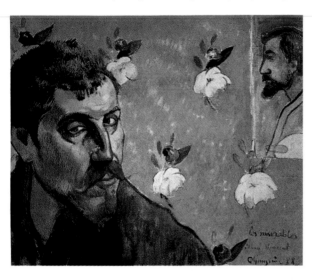

■ Paul Gauguin, *Les Misérables*, 1888, Van Gogh Museum, Amsterdam. In this painting created specifically for van Gogh, Gauguin portrays himself as Jean Valjean, one of the most famous heroes by Victor Hugo, a man forced by his social condition to turn to a life of crime.

■ *Self-Portrait with Bandaged Ear*, 1889, Courtauld Institute, London. In this portrait, painted shortly after his self-mutilation, van Gogh displays dignified composure.

■ Paul Gauguin, *Van Gogh Painting Sun-flowers*, 1888, Vincent Willem van Gogh Collection, Amsterdam. In accordance with Symbolist beliefs in the expressive value of color, Vincent is rendered with the same colors as the flowers.

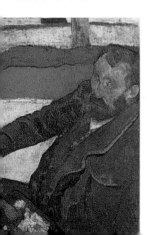

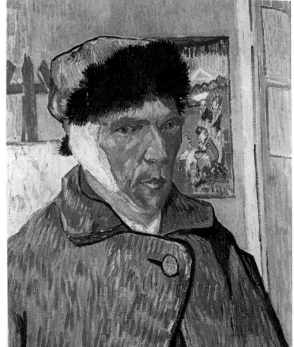

**1888**

# The Artist's Bedroom

Symbolic of his hopes at Arles, Vincent painted this picture of his bedroom in the "Yellow House" in October 1888. He made two more copies of the it while in the asylum. It is now in the Van Gogh Museum in Amsterdam.

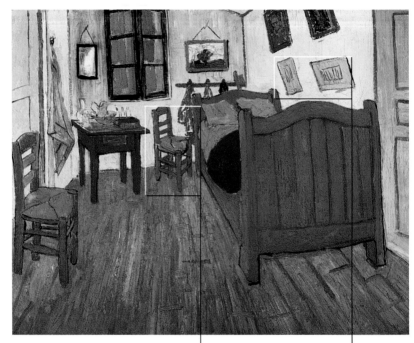

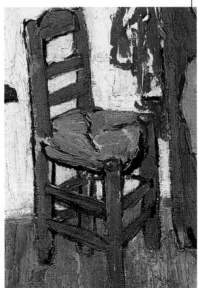

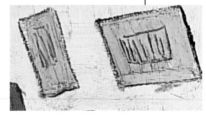

■ Van Gogh's chair was white, but he decided to paint it yellow, because that was the color he associated with the sun, warmth, and happiness.

■ The white walls of the room are portrayed as blue-mauve, a color that agrees with the green of the window, and enhances the yellow of the bed.

■ *Vincent's Bedroom,* 1889, The Art Institute of Chicago. Vincent described his original bedroom picture as "a painting to rest the brain – or the imagination". In this later version, executed in Saint Rémy, the sense of calm is threatened by the sensation of movement in the lines of the floor and bed.

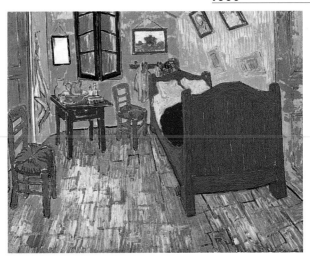

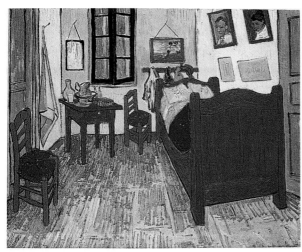

■ *Vincent's Bedroom,* 1889, Musée d'Orsay, Paris. Although no people appear in this picture, there is an air of expectancy. Conceived in anticipation of Gauguin's arrival in October 1888, the painting symbolizes Vincent's hopes that the "Yellow House" would become a base for an artist's colony.

■ In this drawing sent to Theo, Vincent proudly explains the layout of his room. The artist's passionate soul finds an expression in the bowl and the chair, the wall, and the pictures decorating it. Every 20th century artist had to reckon with Vincent's physical representation of his psyche.

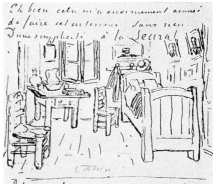

# The Roulin family

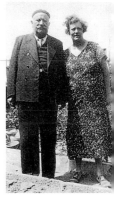

In a letter to his brother Theo, van Gogh wrote: "Roulin, though he is not quite old enough to be like a father to me, nevertheless has a silent gravity and a tenderness for me such as an old soldier might have for a young one." Joseph Roulin was a postman Vincent had probably met in a bistro. He was a good man, and van Gogh was often invited to his house for dinner, a kindness the artist repaid by creating portraits of the whole family. Vincent felt a deep, honest affection for this family, and this enabled him to detect many noble and positive traits in their faces: he believed that Joseph's features were colored by a certain Russian nobility reminiscent of Tolstoy, and he portrayed Armand, the postman's elder son, as a young romantic hero. Roulin supported Vincent through everything, until in 1889 he was transferred to Marseille. In about 1895, an important art dealer named Ambroise Vollard traced the Roulins and persuaded Joseph and his wife to sell the pictures by Vincent that decorated their flat. His paintings therefore ended up in museums all over the world. The Roulins embodied Vincent's last dreams of a family.

■ Taken in 1939, this photograph portrays the handsome Armand and little Marcelle Roulin. Armand's attire is the epitome of Provençal taste.

■ Paul Gauguin, *Portrait of Madame Roulin*, 1888, The Saint Louis Art Museum, Saint Louis. In this portrait, Gauguin gave Augustine's flat, simple face the relaxed features of an exotic mask.

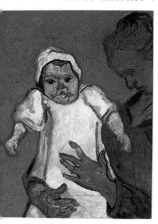

■ *Mother Roulin with Her Baby*, December 1888, The Metropolitan Museum of Art, New York. Marcelle stares with a new-born's gaze. The yellow signifies the warmth of motherhood.

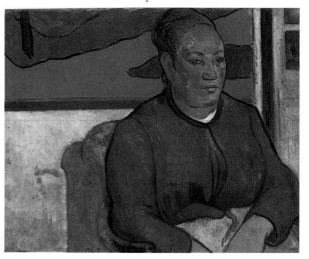

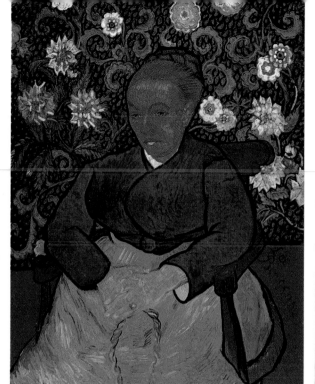

■ *La Berceuse* ("The Lullaby"), 1888, Kröller-Müller Museum, Otterlo. Painted shortly after the birth of Marcelle, this portrait shows Joseph's wife Augustine. The rope she holds on her lap is for rocking the cradle.

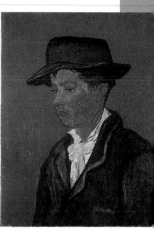

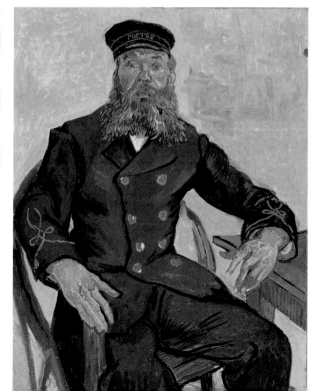

■ *Portrait of Armand Roulin*, December 1888, Museum Boymans van Beuningen, Rotterdam. In this delicate, tender painting of Armand, Vincent portrayed a boy on the threshold between adolescence and young adulthood.

■ *Portrait of Joseph Roulin*, 1888, Museum of Fine Arts, Boston. Although the blue uniform is the dominant element in the painting, Roulin's character emerges more strongly than the officialism of his role. In a letter to Theo, Vincent described him as "neither embittered, nor sad, nor perfect, nor happy, nor always irreproachably just."

**1888**

# The Provence of Mireille and Tartarin

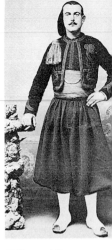

Vincent's fascination with Provence is likely to have started with books. He admired Zola, whose *Stories for Ninon* constitute one of the most poetic representations of life in the south of France, and whose cycle of novels *Les Rougon-Macquart* is partly set in Aix. Van Gogh was also an admirer of Alphonse Daudet: he had especially enjoyed the grotesque saga of *Tartarin de Tarascon*, a humorous satire on southern vanity. Daudet's bitter-sweet realism became popular in his lifetime thanks to his *Lettres de mon moulin*, a best-selling book that combined romantic tales with stories reminiscent of Rabelais. During van Gogh's sojourn in Arles, Provençal literature was enjoying a period of revival brought about by movements eager to promote the old local language and restore its literary dignity, such as the Félibrige current. Frédéric Mistral's works attempted to revive the *langue d'oc*, a language that, although forgotten by official documents, was still very much alive within the local community. Not knowing any *langue d'oc*, Vincent was unable to read the original of the poem *Mireille*. He told Theo that he would like to see the opera Gounod had drawn from it, adding, in a letter in 1889, that on top of everything else, the local language was extremely musical on the lips of the women in Arles.

■ Like a real-life Tartarin, this Zouave soldier poses in his uniform for a photograph. The people of Arles were proud of this costume, since it was a symbol of strength.

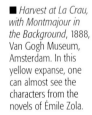

■ *Harvest at La Crau, with Montmajour in the Background*, 1888, Van Gogh Museum, Amsterdam. In this yellow expanse, one can almost see the characters from the novels of Émile Zola.

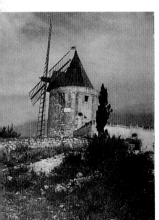

■ This is the famous mill in which the author Alphonse Daudet wrote his *Lettres de mon moulin*.

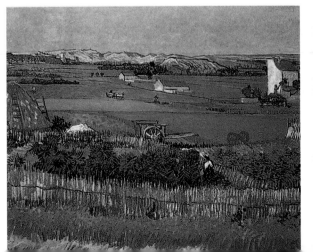

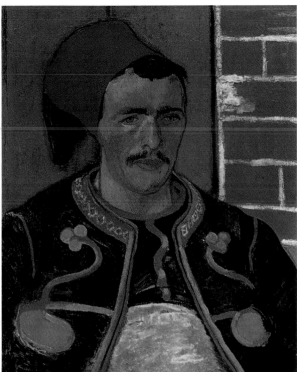

■ *The Zouave*, June 1888, Van Gogh Museum, Amsterdam. The dominating tones of red seem to embody the brutal instincts of the Zouave, but also his sadness. It was not easy for these soldiers to be integrated into the social life of a town.

■ Édouard Manet, *The Fifer*, 1866, Musée d'Orsay, Paris. Vincent was familiar with this painting. Here Manet portrayed military life as an echo of distant wars.

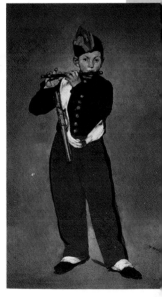

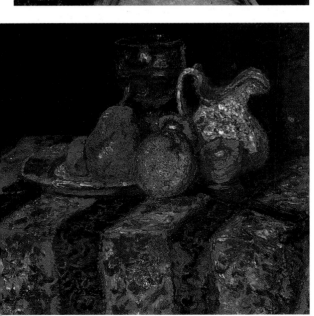

■ Adolphe Monticelli, *Still Life with Rug*, 1878, Musée des Beaux-Arts, Lyon. Vincent was influenced by Monticelli's rich colors and heavy impasto.

**1888**

# The Night Café

"In my picture of the 'Night Café' I have tried to express…the powers of darkness in a low public house." Painted in September 1888, this work now hangs in the Yale University Art Gallery in New Haven.

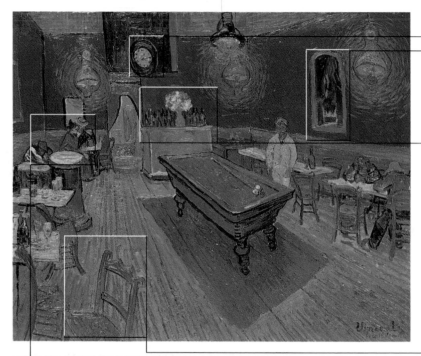

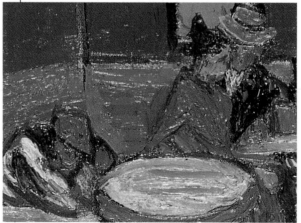

■ In the background, rendered with a dizzy perspective, a couple sits at a table: they are barely sketched, as if they were just another object in the scene. The rough sketching, the interest in physical things, and the moral preoccupation are reminiscent of Vincent's Dutch paintings. He felt this was the French equivalent of *The Potato Eaters*, a work hinted at in the light of the lamps. It is a moving portrayal of social outcasts.

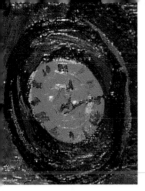

■ A subtle reference to the brevity of life, this clock marks the hours of a night of solitude. Maybe Vincent was inspired by the hourglasses included in many German works as a *memento mori*, a reminder of approaching death.

■ The mirror played a major role in Manet's café interiors, where it was a lively, almost magical element. In this painting, the mirror is a black surface broken by sulphurous reflections.

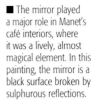

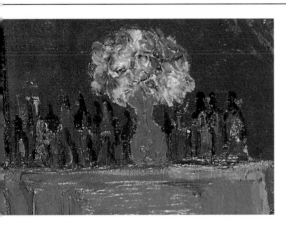

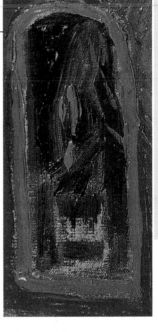

■ The blood-red walls of the café evoke "terrible human passions". Within this atmosphere of "a devil's furnace", the bottles on the bar seem to huddle together, as if seeking safety in numbers.

■ The empty chair is a recurring element in the art of van Gogh, who used it to convey his feelings of isolation.

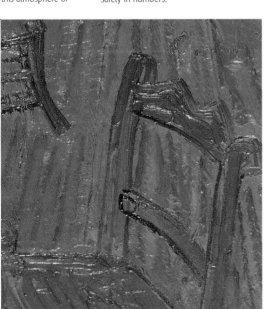

# The palette of the South

■ *Public Park with Weeping Willow: The Poet's Garden I*, September 1888, The Art Institute of Chicago. This canvas portrays a corner of the public park in Arles but, as he was painting it, van Gogh was thinking of Petrarch's garden in Valchiusa. Vincent was surprised to find the same cypresses and oleanders the Italian poet had so loved.

In July 1888, Vincent van Gogh wrote enthusiastically about how Provence had reawakened his lust for life, and claimed that painting was now "extraordinarily exciting". He believed that the colors used by the Impressionists had a tendency to fade, "one more reason for simply making them too bright – in time they will just become dull". He also became convinced that modern art needed to be violently vivid, full of expressive colors, and of lively execution. These beliefs were reflected in his canvases, which burned with bright greens and yellows. Indeed, colors embodied Vincent's challenge against time: he was confident that they, at least, would continue to shine of their own glory, and sing their own praise. Vincent van Gogh's dizzy chromaticism forms the basis of some of the most exhilarating artistic experiments of the 20th century, including Fauvism and Expressionism.

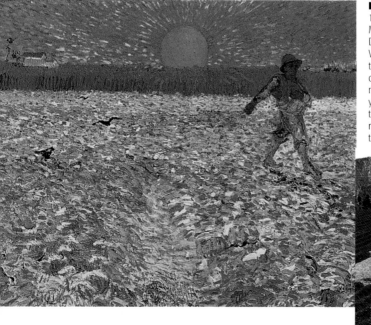

■ *The Sower*, June 1888, Kröller-Müller Museum, Otterlo. During his time at Arles, Vincent often returned to the symbolic theme of the sower. The quasi-mystical force of the yellow sun reinforces the feelings of hope and regeneration created by the actions of the sower.

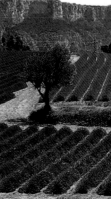

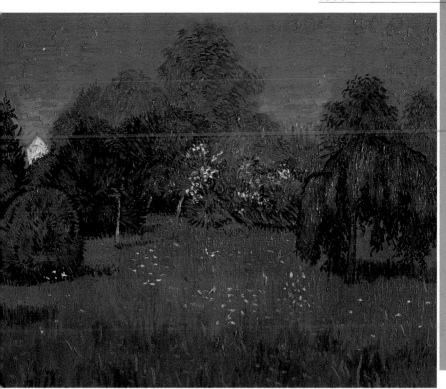

■ The color and perfume of lavender fields fill the streets in Provence. Around the abbeys of Thoronet and Sylvacane the purple of the fields is offset by the silver of the olive trees, creating splendid landscapes.

■ *The Old Mill*, September 1888, Albright-Knox Art Gallery, Buffalo. The thickly applied paint gives this canvas added expressive strength, especially in the spatula strokes in the foreground.

BACKGROUND

# Provence: land of painters

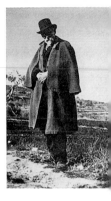

The great Cézanne was born in Aix in 1839. He stopped exhibiting with the Impressionists as early as 1878, when he retired to the south, far from any worldly frivolity. A solitary man and a slow worker, he had been a friend of Zola in his youth. However, after being described in *L'Oeuvre* as a genius who failed to achieve his potential due to an excess of prudence, Cézanne distanced himself from the writer. Finding solace in his art, he started to lead an almost monastic life, which was in direct contradiction to his youthful excesses. Eager to discover the secrets of nature, he was often seen wandering in the countryside around Aix. Only a few years apart, both van Gogh and Cézanne found relief in the solitude of Provençal life. Today, both artists are acknowledged as the forerunners of modern art. Pierre-Auguste Renoir (1841–1919) was also based in the south of France. After a lively Impressionist period, he travelled to Italy, where he was inspired by the draftsmanship of the Italian Renaissance masters. Confident that the light of Provence gave his art greater solidity, Renoir had been travelling to the south since the 1880s. In 1903 he moved permanently to Cagnes-sur-Mer.

■ In the photograph is the "great elder" of Aix, Paul Cézanne. He said: "In painting there are two elements, the eye and the brain, and they must help each other".

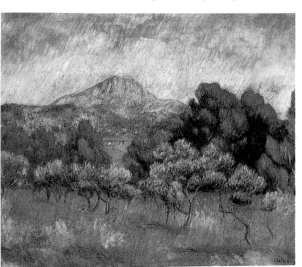

■ Pierre-Auguste Renoir, *Mont Sainte-Victoire*, 1889, University Art Gallery, New Haven. Renoir's take on the mountain of Sainte-Victoire is very different from Cézanne's. A former china decorator, Renoir was an admirer of 17th-century art, especially its grace, pastel tones, and soft and sensuous lines.

## Paul Cézanne

An unsociable, difficult man, Paul Cézanne (1839–1906) was an isolated genius, who often expressed less than flattering comments on Vincent van Gogh's art. Throughout his life, he tried to maintain a freshness of outlook and feeling in his paintings. He also believed in organizing color within the pictorial composition according to an intellectual order. Cézanne said: "Nature should be rendered by means of the cone, the cylinder, and the sphere."

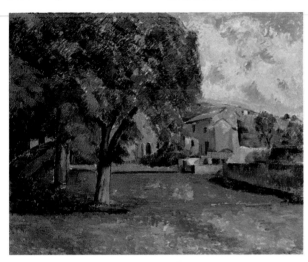

■ Paul Cézanne, *Chestnut Trees and Farmhouse at Jas de Bouffan*, 1885–87, Pushkin Museum, Moscow. In *langue d'oc*, Jas de Bouffon means "realm of the winds": Cézanne lived here with his wife Hortense and son Paul. He used short, oblique touches of color to create volume and space within his canvases.

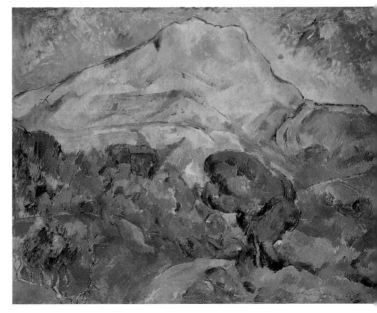

■ Paul Cézanne, *Mont Sainte-Victoire*, 1896–98, The State Hermitage Museum, St. Petersburg. The poet Rilke claimed that "on the plain overlooking Sainte-Victoire, after Cézanne selected it as his model, there shine more stars than anywhere else". Cézanne was certainly inspired by the many ways in which Hokusai had portrayed Mount Fujiyama. Unlike the Japanese artist, however, Cézanne did not want to represent the rocky giant as an ephemeral, contingent entity, but as an eternal, all-encompassing one that included different times and seasons.

**1888**

# The Café Terrace at Night

Vincent painted this café on the Place du Forum at Arles in September 1888. Although created at about the same time as the *Night Café*, this colorful exterior is a less dramatic work. It is now in the Kröller-Müller Museum in Otterlo.

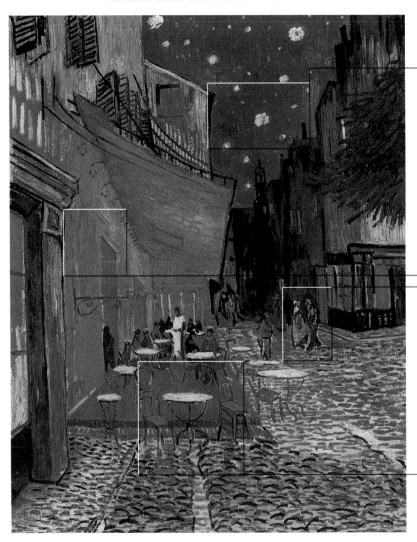

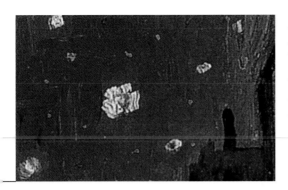

■ In this painting Vincent portrayed the stars as heavenly flowers. Conversely, Henri Matisse later said that flowers are stars on earth. In a letter to Wilhelmina, Vincent wrote: "…here is a night picture without any black, nothing but beautiful blue and violet and green".

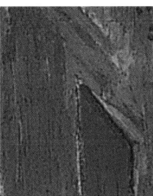

■ The "sulphur yellow" of the lighted terrace, is enhanced by the blue of the street receding into the distance and the purple-blue of the door frame in the foreground. Within a few centimeters of canvas, the cobblestones turn from deep green to bright orange.

■ Enveloped in the warm, joyful light of the café, the passers-by on the Place du Forum seem to acknowledge one another. On the right-hand side of the painting, a woman with a bonnet and shawl walks past a man with his hands in his pockets.

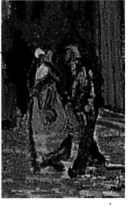

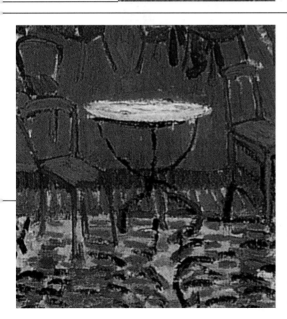

■ Shiny as silver coins, the tables of the café seem to call the passers-by. Placed next to each other, they resemble full moons in the summer, especially for the way in which they reflect the lights of the night.

**1888**

# A visit to Saintes-Maries-de-la-Mer

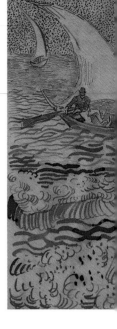

In May 1888, van Gogh planned a trip to Saintes-Maries-de-la-Mer, 50 kilometers (31 miles) from Arles. He wrote that the only way to travel was "by diligence" through Camargue, which he described as "a large expanse of grass, with herds of fighting bulls and beautiful wild horses." He went the following month, writing to Theo that the Camargue seemed to him like a landscape by Ruysdaël. At the end of the 19th century, Saintes-Maries-de-la-Mer was a poor fishing village. Vincent was surprised that there were no cliffs, but sandy beaches like the ones in Holland, and compared the changing hue of the sea to that of mackerels. He felt that one could never define its color completely, whether green, purple, or blue because, in an instant, a fleeting reflection gave it a pink or grey shade. The unusual name of the most famous village in Camargue derives from a legend according to which Mary Jacob, sister of the Virgin Mary, Mary Salome, their servant Sarah, Lazarus, Martha, and Mary Magdalene, forced to flee from Judea, landed here. The remains of Mary Jacob, Mary Salome and Sarah were allegedly found in 1448 during the excavations commissioned by King René. The great pilgrimage of May 24 and 25 start from here.

■ "Beautiful Saint, Queen of this valley of tears, fill our nets with fish, if you please" These are the last lines of the story of Mireille. This statue in Saintes-Maries-de-la-Mer is dedicated to the heroine created by Mistral.

■ *Street in Saintes-Maries-de-la-Mer*, 1888, Private Collection. The huts with straw roofs typical of Camargue are called *mas*. Drawn with a reed pen, this sketch demonstrates Vincent's technical virtuosity: he no longer needed the perspective frame used in his earlier works.

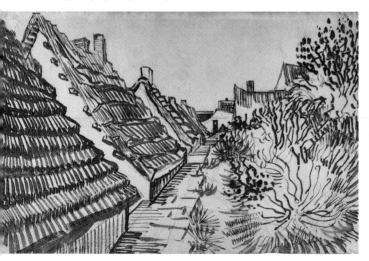

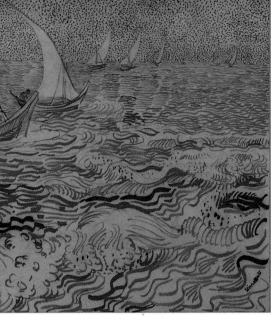

■ *Seascape at Saintes-Maries-de-la-Mer*, 1888, Musée d'Art Moderne, Brussels. Inspired by the painting shown below, this sketch was sent to John Russell. As in all sketches addressed to him, Vincent rendered the sky by a multitude of tiny dots.

■ *Seascape at Saintes-Maries-de-la-Mer*, 1888, Pushkin Museum, Moscow. Van Gogh was pleased with this small painting, and signed it in the bottom right-hand corner. In a letter to Bernard he wrote that the boats were so lovely they resembled flowers.

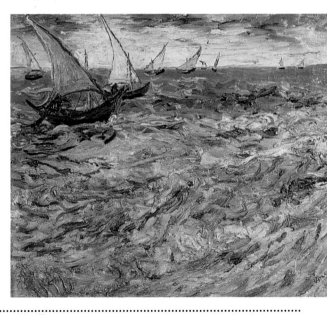

## Mireille

The story of Mireille, the heroine of Mistral's 1859 eponymous poem, is a sad one. After making a votive offering to be able to see her beloved, Mireille has to go on a lonely pilgrimage to the sanctuary of the Virgin Mary. Overwhelmed by anxiety, however, she dies by the altar. The story was set to music by Gounod in an opera influenced by the singing of Provençal troubadours.

**1888**

# "Figures as beautiful as those of Goya or Velázquez"

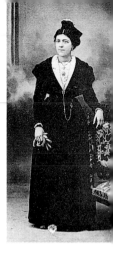

On July 31, 1888, Vincent wrote that what he really liked about the area were "the colorful clothes: the women and girls dress in cheap, simple material, green, red, pink, yellow, havana brown, purple, blue, polka-dots, stripes. White scarves, red, green, and yellow parasols. A strong sulphurous sun shines down on it all". The word *Arlésienne* immediately evokes, and must have done even more so in Vincent's time, a novel by Alphonse Daudet that Georges Bizet set to music in 1872 – a tragic story of love and death told with unusual terseness, as if the real protagonist was fate itself. In van Gogh's paintings, the women of Arles often convey the same severe strength found in Daudet's novel. The subject of this series of works is the owner of the Café de la Gare, Madame Ginoux (1848–1911), whose strong features recall ancient sculptures. Vincent felt that people are the root of everything and that painting figures allowed him to cultivate the best part of himself. He wrote that he was keen on vertical female figures, and that he had met a man familiar with Spain and its art who said his *Arlésienne* was as beautiful as a painting by the great Spanish artists.

■ This photograph portrays an Arlesian woman. Vincent wrote about their beauty in a letter of February 25, 1888. Guided by literature, Vincent saw in the women of Arles the colors of Velázquez and the elegant sensuality of some figures by Goya.

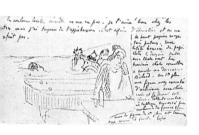

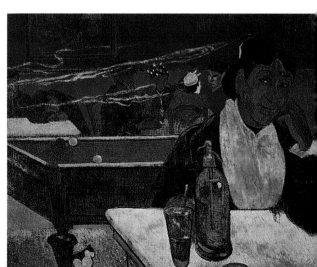

■ Paul Gauguin, sketch for *At the Café*, 1888, location unknown. In the background of the sketch there are three prostitutes and two Zouaves, one sleeping off his drunkenness on the table. The figure of the black and white cat squatting under the billiard table recalls oriental prints.

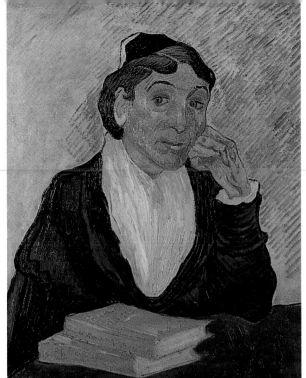

■ *L'Arlésienne (Madame Ginoux)*, February 1890, Museu de Arte, São Paulo. Vincent returned to the subject of the *Arlésienne* during his hospitalization in Saint-Rémy. His starting point was the painting by Gauguin that he had kept as a bitter reminder of a failed experiment.

■ *L'Arlésienne: Madame Ginoux with Books*, November 1888, The Metropolitan Museum of Art, New York. Marie Ginoux and her husband owned the Café de la Gare near the "Yellow House". Born in 1848, she died in 1911.

■ Paul Gauguin, *At the Café*, 1888, Pushkin Museum, Moscow. Gauguin wrote to Bernard: "I painted a café that Vincent loves, although I do not like it much. It is not my style: the local colors of some bar do not appeal to me. It is a matter of education that cannot be changed".

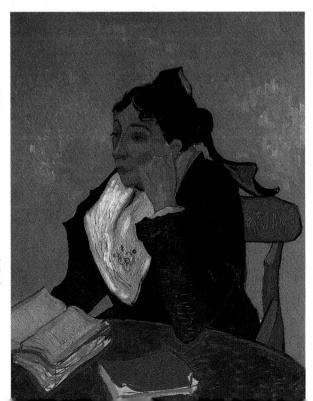

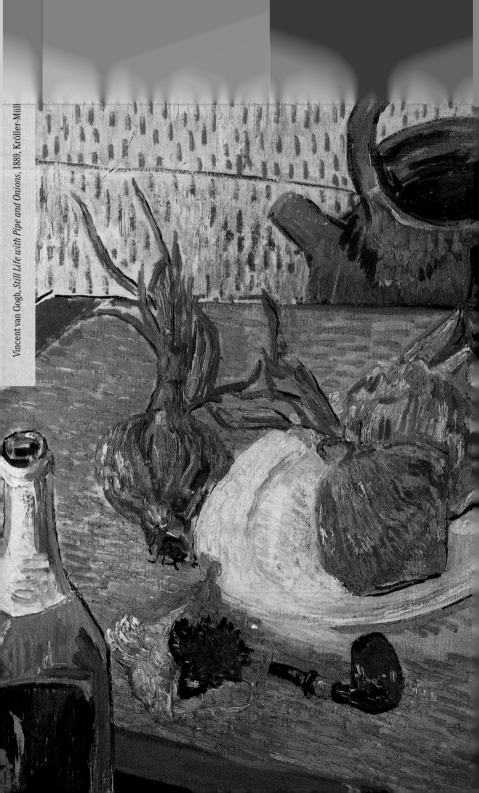

Vincent van Gogh, *Still Life with Pipe and Onions*, 1889, Kröller-Müll

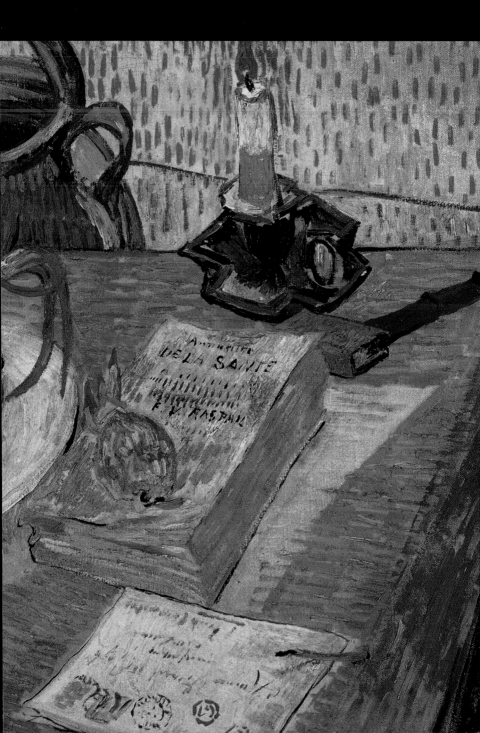

**1889**

# The confinement

Čhroni...

Ⓞn December 24, Vincent was taken to the Hotel-Dieu in Arles, where he was put in the hands of Doctor Félix Rey. Against Vincent's wishes, Gauguin summoned Theo from Paris. On January 4 he was visited by the faithful Roulin and by Salles, the local pastor, who was instrumental in ensuring his temporary release. On February 7 he was taken back to the hospital suffering from delusions. This time, petitioned by the citizens of Arles, the door of the "Yellow House" was sealed by the police. In March, aided by Paul Signac, who had travelled to Arles to visit him, Vincent forced the door to enter the "Yellow House" for the last time. He presented Signac with a still life of two herrings. After Theo's wedding on April 17, Vincent agreed to be admitted at an asylum at nearby Saint-Rémy. He became a clinical case, with doctors and critics unable to reach a definite diagnosis. Some suspected paranoia and manic depression, while others blamed venereal diseases and alcoholic excesses. Psychoanalysts traced the reasons behind Vincent's drama to a guilt complex deriving from the death of his older brother and to his desperate need for love. But poets like Artaud saw a parallel with the condition of Beethoven and Hölderlin, for whom madness was the result of the struggle between the creative soul and bourgeois philistinism.

■ This cutting from a local newspaper narrates Vincent van Gogh's drama.

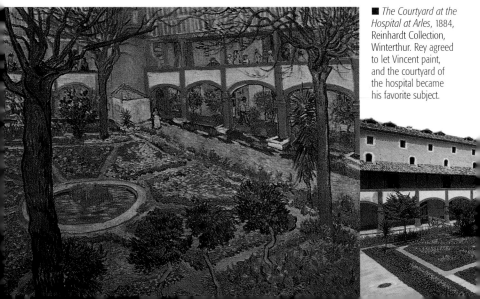

■ *The Courtyard at the Hospital at Arles*, 1884, Reinhardt Collection, Winterthur. Rey agreed to let Vincent paint, and the courtyard of the hospital became his favorite subject.

## e locale

à 11 heures 1|2 du
augogh. peintre, o-
st pré-enté à la mai-
1, a demandé la
remis. . . . son o-
rdez cet objet pré-
»aru. Informée de ce
que celui d'un pau-
ren-lue le lendemain
qu'elle a trouvé cou-
nt pre-que plus signe

admis d'urgence à

■ Doctor Félix Rey
looked after van Gogh
in Arles from December
24, 1888 until January 7,
1889. He diagnosed a
severe epileptic disorder.

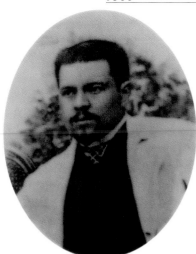

■ *Portrait of Doctor
Félix Rey*, January
1889, Pushkin Museum,
Moscow. Félix Rey
(1867–1932) was
given this painting by
Vincent as a present.
He subsequently sold
it to an art dealer in
Marseille who was
probably acting on
behalf of the famous
Vollard. It was Vollard
who sold the picture to
a Russian art collector.

■ As shown by this
recent photograph, the
courtyard of the hospital
in Arles has not changed
since the time of
Vincent's hospitalization.
The building now
houses an exhibition
of van Gogh's works.

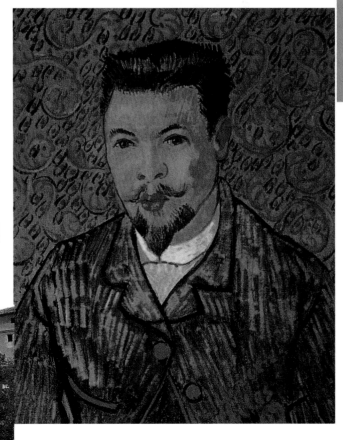

**1889**

# Self-Portrait with Bandaged Ear

Painted in January 1889, this work is the tragic
testimony of the passionate story of affection,
rage, and disappointment Vincent had with Paul
Gauguin. It is part of a private collection.

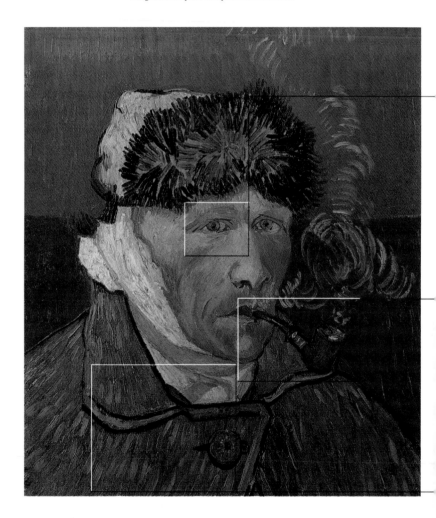

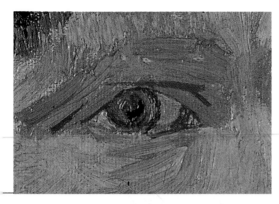

■ Van Gogh's expression reminds one of the opening lines of Baudelaire's *Les fleurs du mal*: "You, hypocritical reader, who are my brother and my fellow man". The red in his eyes seems to reflect the background and, although not actually represented, evokes the idea of blood.

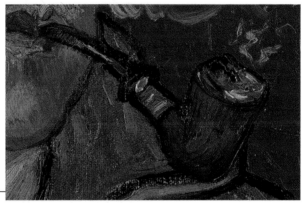

■ The pipe was one of Vincent's most cherished possessions, especially in his most difficult moments: even on his deathbed, he held one between his teeth. Here it is the symbol of his newly-found lucidity.

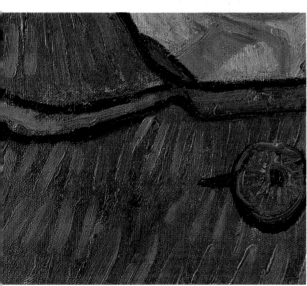

■ Although this is a rather conventional composition – a triangle anchored at the two bottom corners of the canvas – the coloring of the painting is very dynamic: the black outlines seem barely to contain the outbursts of color. The dark green of the threadbare coat is rendered with thick, parallel strokes: the green contrasting sharply with its complementary red.

**1889**

# Vincent's flowers

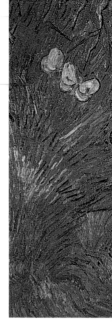

Ever since his childhood, Vincent had loved flowers, birds, and insects, and impressed his family with his ability to draw plants and landscapes. He was especially fond of birds' nests, which he associated with the protective family circle. His favorite plants were also the most discreet, those that live and thrive without any interference from man. Vincent believed that a painter should draw a weeping willow as if it was a human being, and that concentrated observation was the key to portraying nature sympathetically. "Nature always opposes the artist, but whoever takes art seriously will not let this resistance discourage him". Vincent van Gogh felt that he had established a privileged mutual rapport with nature and, in a letter to his brother Theo, wrote about his ambition to decorate his studio in Arles with "some six paintings of sunflowers, a decor in which the vivid or broken chrome yellows will stand out sharply against various blue backgrounds, from the palest Veronese green to royal blue, in a frame of thin slats painted in red lead. The kind of subject you would see on the windows of Gothic cathedrals".

■ *Two White Butterflies*, 1889, Van Gogh Museum, Amsterdam. Vincent enjoyed observing and studying insects. Yoshimaro's *A new book of insects* inspired him to look even closer at the microcosm in the fields.

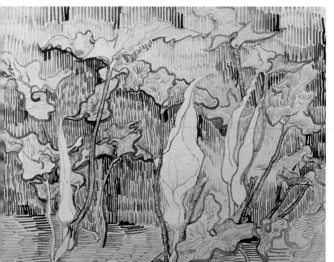

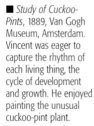

■ *Study of Cuckoo-Pints*, 1889, Van Gogh Museum, Amsterdam. Vincent was eager to capture the rhythm of each living thing, the cycle of development and growth. He enjoyed painting the unusual cuckoo-pint plant.

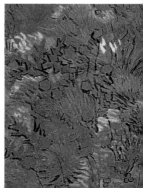

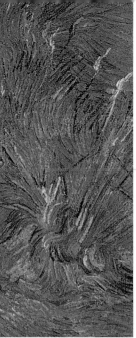

■ *Clumps of Grass*, April 1889, Private Collection, Japan. Like a Japanese artist, Vincent wanted to approach the infinitely small details of nature, and feel the forces of the universe pulse within them. He spent hours lying on the grass, feeling its smell and texture.

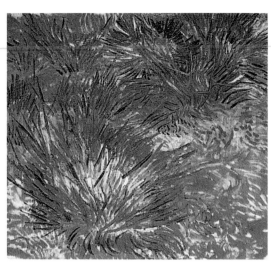

■ *Still Life: Vase with Fourteen Sunflowers*, 1888, Van Gogh Museum, Amsterdam. "Peonies are Jeannin's, hollyhocks are Quost's, and sunflowers are mine", wrote Vincent to Theo in 1889.

■ *A Field of Yellow Flowers*, 1889, Kunstmuseum, Winterthur. This is a series of dizzy variations on yellows, with the odd touch of green achieved by adding a few strokes of blue to the sunny triumph of the painting.

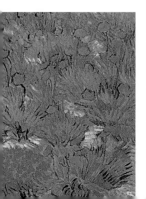

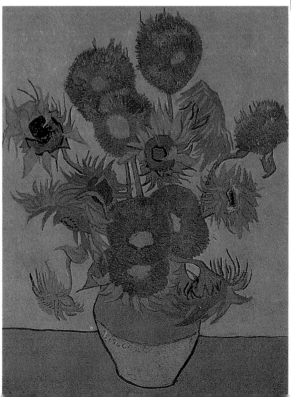

**1889**

# My dear Bernard,…

O ne of Vincent's most regular correspondents was Émile Bernard, whom he had met in Cormon's studio. Born in Lille in 1868, Bernard was the forerunner of many modern artistic currents. He flirted with divisionism, but soon came to believe that fragmenting color meant sacrificing its intensity. Together with Louis Anquetin, he developed a style in which large flat areas of color are enclosed within bold, dark outlines. This technique, known as Cloisonnism, was inspired by medieval stained-glass and cloisonné enamel. Bernard and Gauguin experimented with this artistic expression during their stay in Pont-Aven. In the preface to the collection of van Gogh letters published by Vollard in 1911, Bernard wrote about Vincent: "As a sketcher, he was eager to draw the fingers of a hand without portraying them as the forceps they look so much like; as a colorist, he was often unable to find the right chromatic balance; but, always and everywhere, he handled solid matter with expressive frenzy". Bernard died in Paris in 1911.

■ Henri de Toulouse-Lautrec, *Portrait of Émile Bernard*, 1886, Tate Gallery, London. Although van Gogh did not agree with Bernard's decision to focus on a style of elegant abstraction, the rapport between the two artists remained strong. Vincent played a father-figure to Bernard, who published van Gogh's letters in the *Mercure de France*.

■ Émile Bernard, *Still Life with Vases and Apples*, 1887, Musée National d'Art Moderne, Paris. A perfect example of decorative Synthetism, this painting is clearly influenced by Gauguin's teachings in Pont-Aven: the colors are used symbolically to represent the tradition and religious spirit of peasants. Bernard's interest in stained glass and Japanese art is evident in the areas of flat color.

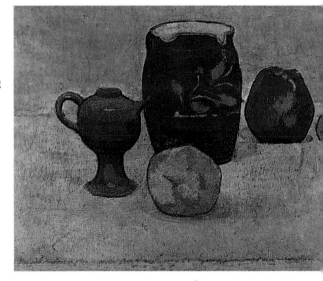

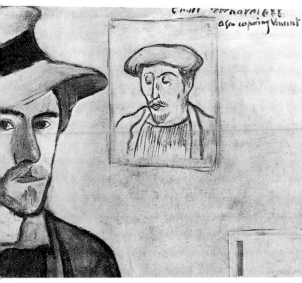

■ Émile Bernard, *Self-Portrait Dedicated to van Gogh*, 1888, Van Gogh Museum, Amsterdam. Vincent wrote of receiving this self-portrait by Bernard as well as one by Gauguin. Each artist included a sketch of the other in his work. Van Gogh felt that Gauguin's work was remarkable, but preferred the honesty of Bernard's.

■ *Breton Women* (after Émile Bernard), 1888, Civica Galleria d'Arte Moderna, Collezione Grassi, Milan. Gauguin brought Bernard's painting to Arles, where Vincent, who was impressed by it, made this copy. However, van Gogh was struck not so much by the religious meaning (the painting portrayed a *pardon*, that is a popular procession), but by the beauty of the composition and the naïve, yet definite color.

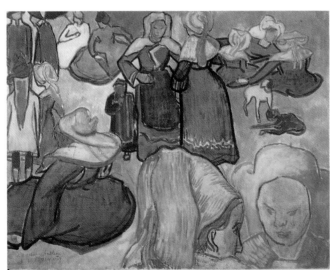

### The Pont-Aven School

This was the name adopted by a group of artists gathered in the inn of Marie-Jeanne Gloanec at Pont-Aven, near the Breton coast. The School centred around Gauguin and Bernard. Gauguin moved there first, finding a small community of Danish, American, and English intellectuals. Soon he was joined by Paul Sérusier and Charles Laval. The Pont-Aven School reacted to Impressionism by promoting a simplified synthesis of colors. The works of these artists recall the visual effects of stained-glass.

**1889**

# Road with Cypress and Star

While at Saint-Rémy, Vincent painted a series featuring cypress trees. He told Theo they were "as beautiful as an Egyptian obelisk…a splash of black in a sunny landscape". This work is now in the Kröller-Müller Museum in Otterlo.

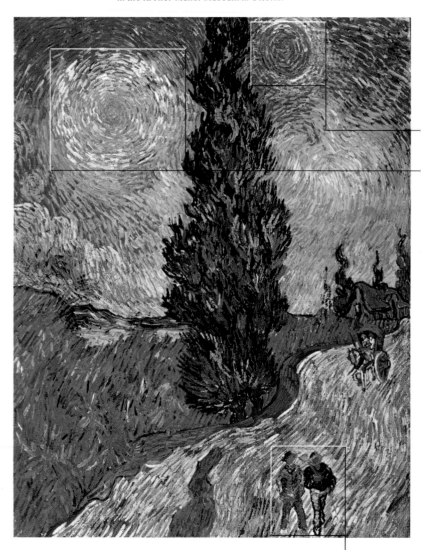

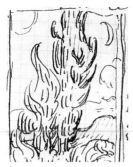

■ Vincent sketched this cypress in a letter. It resembles a flame rising to the sky.

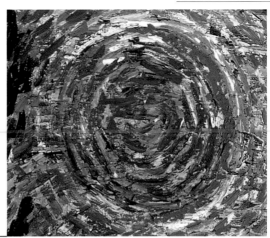

■ The sky vibrates with a sense of urgency and tension. The cypress, traditionally seen as a symbol of death, acts as the focal point around which the lines sweep and swirl in a powerful expression of the forces of nature. The moon and the stars are recurring motifs in van Gogh's work.

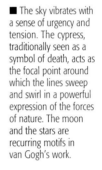

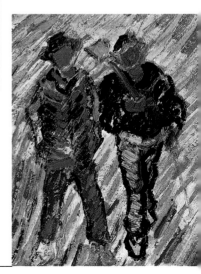

■ Van Gogh painted the stars with a halo of yellow, green, and white brushstrokes on the background of a sky that is turning to dusk.

■ The figures of the two men and the approaching carriage are minute compared to the large cypress. They seem lost in the immensity of the cosmic movement that surrounds and flows around them.

**1889**

# Saint-Rémy

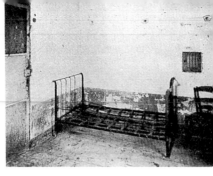

"I saw Vincent again, last time I was in Arles, in the Spring of 1889. He was already an inmate at the town hospital. All day long we talked about painting, literature, and socialism." Thus wrote Paul Signac, the last person to see van Gogh in Arles. In May 1889 Vincent agreed to be hospitalized again. Pastor Salles found him a place at the asylum in Saint-Paul-de-Mausole, where he was placed in the care of Doctor Peyron. Founded at the beginning of the century by Doctor Mercurin, this ancient monastery was originally an institution with a pleasant park and many other amenities. But things had radically changed in the course of time and, when van Gogh arrived, the building was in a state of neglect. Doctor Peyron gave the artist a single room and allowed him to use a small room in the basement as his studio. From the window, reinforced with iron bars, Vincent could see "a fenced-off wheat field, a typical van Goyen prospect". After Theo's wedding in April, Vincent began to feel increasingly concerned of being a burden to his brother: this was the main reason for agreeing to be hospitalized in Saint-Rémy. As the weather grew milder, towards the end of spring, he began to feel more energetic, and this was reflected in his attitude towards painting. He used to wake up at six in the morning and go out, followed by a guardian, to paint hedges, mountains, and skies.

■ In the picture is a room at the hospital of Saint-Rémy. While van Gogh was here, Theo told him that his wife was expecting, and asked him to be the baby's godfather. Vincent replied that, to deal with this role, he would have to get better first, and asked his brother to call the baby Theodorus.

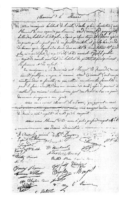

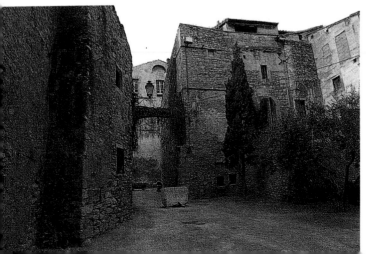

■ At the foot of the northern Alpilles, Saint-Rémy lies by the ancient town of Glanum, famous for the mausoleum erected by Julius Caesar for his nephews. The Aurelian road joining Italy and Spain used to go through here. The medieval village is still charming.

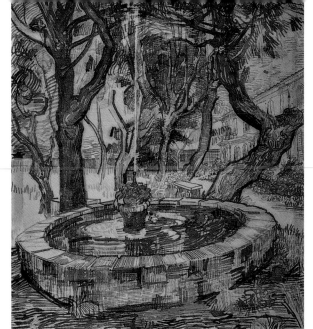

■ *Fountain in the Garden of Saint-Paul Hospital*, 1889, Van Gogh Museum, Amsterdam. The overgrown garden of the hospital in Saint-Rémy became Vincent's microcosm, the world within which he could find his sanity. Van Gogh painted it time and again, and his pictures enable us to be familiar with each corner of the park. This drawing reveals a good knowledge of Cézanne's techniques.

■ Van Gogh believed that the people of Arles still felt a considerable degree of superstition and fear with regards to artists. A petition to have him hospitalized again was signed by 30 inhabitants of his quarter, who believed him to be dangerous.

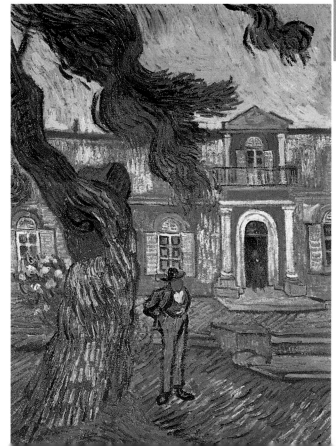

■ *Pine Trees with Figure in the Garden of Saint-Paul Hospital*, 1889, Musée d'Orsay, Paris. Vincent believed that the objective of his art was to capture the spirit of the earth and the sun, the intelligence of man, the essence of the cypress tree, the vineyard, and the olive grove. His trees appear to be tormented like trapped souls, and they tower with their strength above any other figure standing by them.

**1889**

# Still Life with Irises

During his stay at Saint-Rémy, Vincent had many relapses. "I need some air, I feel overwhelmed by boredom and grief", he wrote to Theo. This painting is housed in the Van Gogh Museum in Amsterdam.

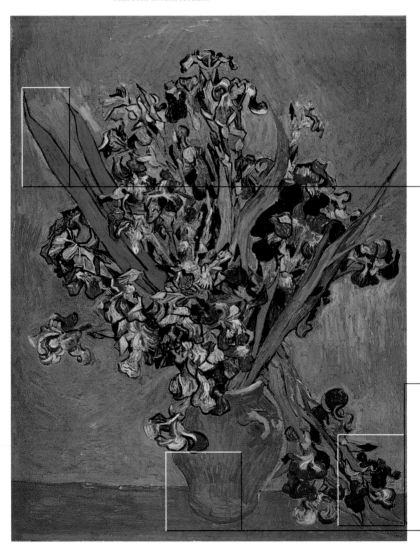

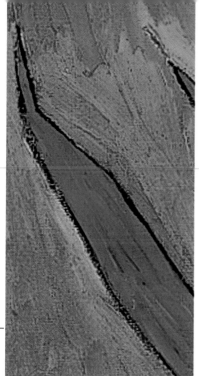

■ The slender, sword-like leaves of the irises are juxtaposed with the velvety richness of the flowers, portrayed by Vincent in all their fragile beauty. The flowers are acutely obsered and painted with meticulous attention to detail: they each have their own individual identity.

Van Gogh paid the same attention to his flower paintings as he did to his portraits. "I am painting a purple bunch that moves through crimson to pure Prussian blue, on a bright lemon yellow background, with other yellow tones in the vase".

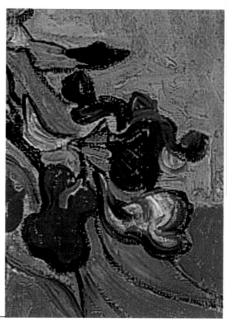

■ Irises had been portrayed in a work kept at the Uffizi, the *Portinari Triptych*. This triptych was the work of Hugo van der Goes (1440–82), a Flemish painter who, having retired when he was only 35 to live in a monastery, had subsequently become insane. Van Gogh was familiar with his story, and mentioned it several times in his letters.

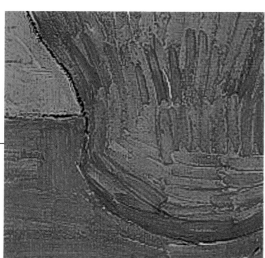

■ The bottom part of the painting is an explosion of yellows. The lemon background envelops the irises and reflects the cold range of their colors. Vincent had already used the exciting chromatic contrast of purple and yellow in *The Sower*. The vase seems to be overcome by the sheer weight of the flowers.

# Landscapes of the Alpilles

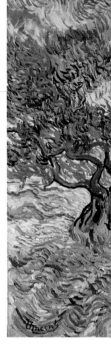

From Orgon to Saint-Gabriel, the ancient town the Romans called Ernaginum, the landscape is dominated by the mountain range of the Alpilles. Rising above the plain of the river Rhône, the Alpilles are the spine of Provence, and they create a beautiful, rugged landscape. This is the land of the tree "by the ancient murmuring sound", as Vincent said, the area where Nostradamus wandered, searching for aromatic herbs. The unusual shape of the rocks, olive groves, and bushes, the buzz of the cicadas, and the sound of the blowing wind have contributed to the creation of many legends in this area. Vincent often walked to an isolated spot, deep in the countryside, where the strong color contrasts of this rugged environment suited and reflected his temperament. During the time he spent at Saint-Rémy, Vincent read Fyodor Dostoyevsky's *Notes from the Underground*, one of the first novels to deal with the psychological research of the unconscious. The anxiety of those pages was perfectly reflected in the tormented landscape of the Alpilles.

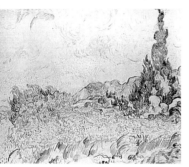

■ *The Road Menders*, November 1889, The Cleveland Museum of Art, Cleveland. In the middle of a road disembowelled by excavations, the strength of nature is reasserted by the huge tree trunks. They turn a mundane urban scene into a world of apocalyptic disarray.

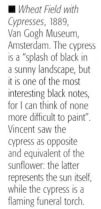

■ *Wheat Field with Cypresses*, 1889, Van Gogh Museum, Amsterdam. The cypress is a "splash of black in a sunny landscape, but it is one of the most interesting black notes, for I can think of none more difficult to paint". Vincent saw the cypress as opposite and equivalent of the sunflower: the latter represents the sun itself, while the cypress is a flaming funeral torch.

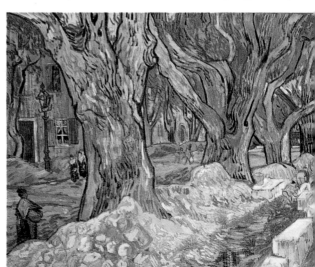

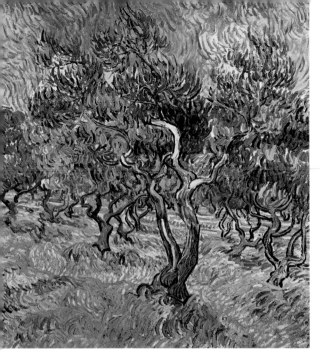

■ *Olive Grove*, 1889, Kröller-Müller Museum, Otterlo. Vincent was fascinated by the shape of olive trees and by the unusual silver tones, which he tried to capture in his paintings. In this picture, he removed the emphasis from the chromatic celebration, to place it on the dynamism of the forms and lines. The shining surfaces of chrome and cobalt blue give way to more sedate tones of grey and ochre.

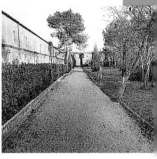

■ *The Garden of Saint-Paul Hospital*, 1889, Folkwang Museum, Essen. While in Saint-Rémy, van Gogh often painted tiny human figures next to large trees to reflect his sense of solitude and anxiety. The real subject here is the broken trunk in the foreground.

■ The wall enclosing the hospital courtyard seems to reflect the duality between the desire to be free and fear of the unknown.

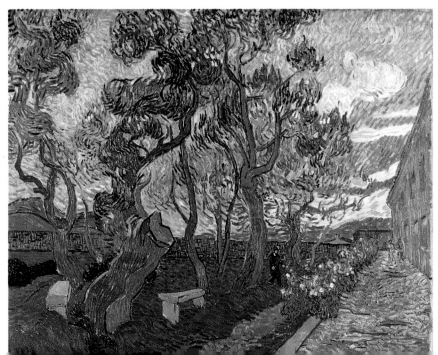

# Starry Night

Vincent sent this painting, together with *Still Life with Irises* (pp. 102–103), to the 1889 Salon des Indépendants, where it was viewed with some bewilderment. The painting is now in the Museum of Modern Art in New York.

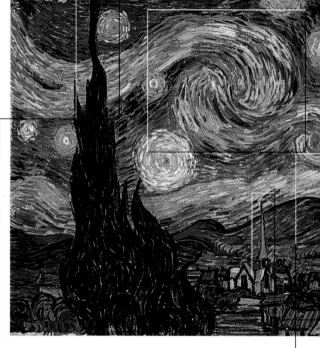

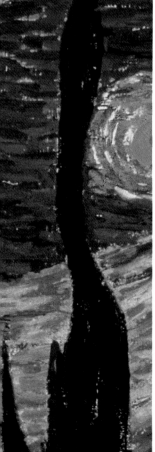

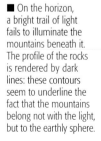

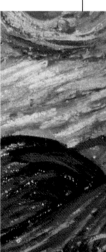

■ The cypresses represent the link between sky and earth, life and death. The slender, gentle trees that had been painted by 15th-century artists with meticulous detail, are turned into dark flames rising to the sky.

■ On the horizon, a bright trail of light fails to illuminate the mountains beneath it. The profile of the rocks is rendered by dark lines: these contours seem to underline the fact that the mountains belong not with the light, but to the earthly sphere.

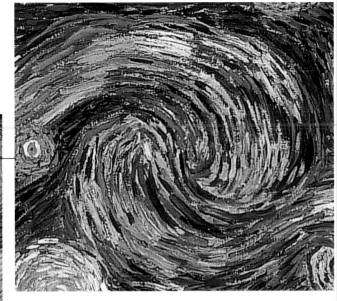

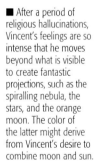

■ After a period of religious hallucinations, Vincent's feelings are so intense that he moves beyond what is visible to create fantastic projections, such as the spiralling nebula, the stars, and the orange moon. The color of the latter might derive from Vincent's desire to combine moon and sun.

■ Van Gogh mixed the landscape of Saint-Rémy with the Dutch villages of his youth. Tall steeples, common in the plains of the north, are rarely seen in the Mediterranean landscape. Vincent was growing increasingly nostalgic for his homeland.

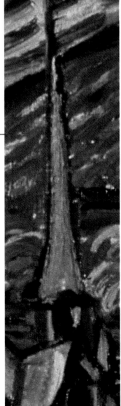

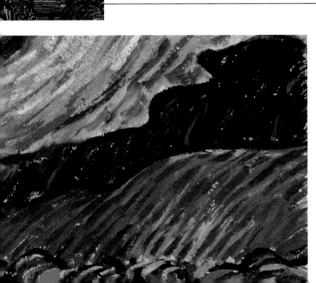

# The developments of his contemporaries

■ Paul Signac, *Saint-Briac*, 1890, Pushkin Museum, Moscow. Signac (1863–1935) was one of Seurat's most dedicated supporters, ardently applying his divisionist techniques.

At the end of the 1880s, the art world was characterized by the development of pointillist, or divisionist, theories: van Gogh had been interested in these techniques since 1886, when he had seen *A Sunday on La Grande Jatte* by Georges Seurat (1859–91). If the Impressionists had adapted artistic expressions to the spirit of the age they were living in, Seurat went even further. He dreamed of a scientific art based on treaties on optics and color perception, an art in which forms and colors were subordinated to the laws of rational harmony. He approached the division of tones in a systematic way, and tried to create atmospheric effects around his subjects. Paul Signac met Seurat in 1884 and took an interest in his theories. He readily adopted Seurat's scientific principles, but later developed a broader, more colorful interpretation. An important development was introduced by the French painter Henri Rousseau, known as the "Dounanier" because of his job in the Paris Customs Office. In about 1886, he stopped creating oleographs of Arcadian landscapes to dedicate himself to a more original art that made him unmistakable.

■ Caran d'Ache, Poster for the Russian Exhibition, 1895, Bibliothèque des Arts Décoratifs, Paris. The late 1880s were golden years for illustrators, from Toulouse-Lautrec and Caran d'Ache, to Steinlen and Bonnard.

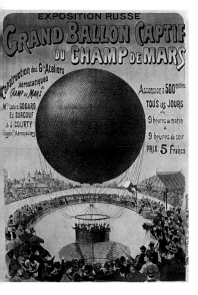

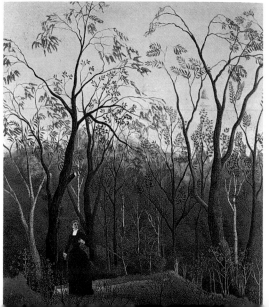

■ Henri Rousseau, *A Walk in the Forest*, 1886, Kunsthaus, Zürich. Pervaded by a romantic feeling of nostalgia, this painting reveals its oneiric quality in the refined rendering of the branches, as fine as lace.

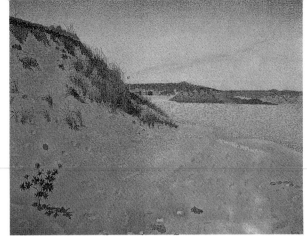

■ Georges Seurat, *Bathers at Asnières*, detail, 1883–84, Tate Gallery, London. Following Rood's theories on optics and Chevreul's laws on complementary colors, Seurat created some masterpieces of pointillism. Vincent wrote: "I often think about Seurat's method, yet I don't follow it at all. The Pointillists have found something new, and anyway I like them a lot".

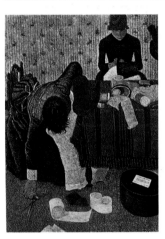

■ Paul Signac, *Milliners*, 1885, Bührle Collection, Zürich. In this painting, Signac applied pointillist theories to an interior for the first time.

■ Paul Signac, *Saint-Tropez*, 1897, Musée de l'Annonciade, Saint-Tropez. Enchanted by the Mediterranean, Signac invited Vincent to join him. By now, however, van Gogh wanted to return to the north of Europe.

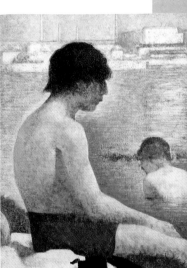

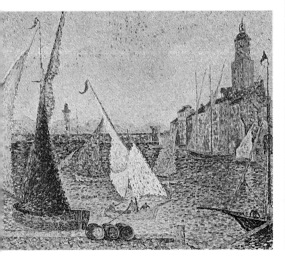

## Georges Seurat

In 1886 Seurat's famous painting *A Sunday on La Grande Jatte*, now in the Art Institute of Chicago, aroused the interest of the public and critics at the final Impressionist exhibition. Paul Signac greatly admired this work, and wrote that, for the first time, an artist had created a canvas painted exclusively with pure colors separated into dots that were mixed by the eye into a whole.

**1889**

# Prisoners Exercising

Painted in 1890, this work is currently housed in the Pushkin Museum in Moscow. Vincent was inspired by an engraving by Gustave Doré that Theo had sent him while he was in the hospital at Arles.

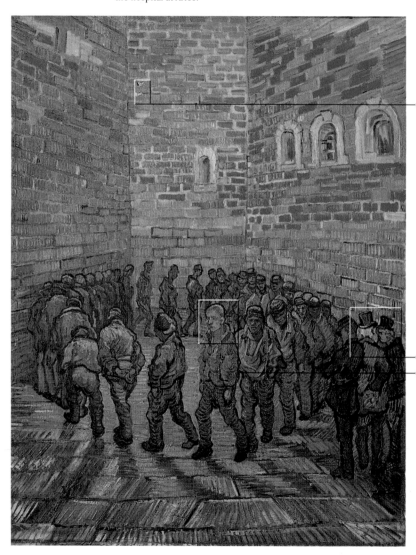

■ In this depressing pit protected by endlessly high walls, there is the flutter of two white butterflies that fly keeping close to each other. They are easily missed at first glance, and are an embodiment of hope, or maybe the nostalgic symbol of a freedom now irrevocably lost. The black and white of Doré's engraving is lyrically translated into a delicate chromatic texture. It is as if van Gogh used a precise, methodic sketching in an attempt to exercise control over the self-destructiveness that was undermining his mind.

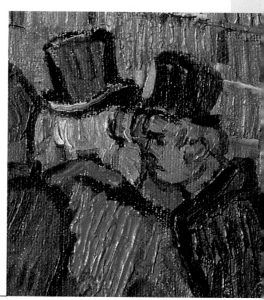

■ The men in the top hats seem to belong in a Daumier engraving: they are observers rather than warders, and seem indifferent to the endless walk of the wretched men in front of them. Their bourgeois reality is juxtaposed with the sorrow of the prisoners. Vincent gave a new interpretation of Doré's image: to him it was the embodiment of his own sense of claustrophobic confinement and desire to escape. This circular walk was a metaphor for his existence, which he lived with a heavy sense of guilt and a passionate desire for freedom.

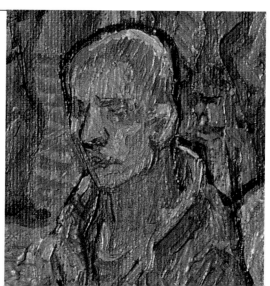

■ Some critics see Vincent's self-portrait in the young blond man in the foreground of the picture. The artist has definitely singled out this character, the only prisoner without a hat. Turned slightly towards the viewer, he looks like he might break free of the circle.

# Working to escape
# from evil

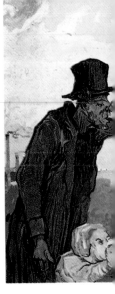

Due to the lack of willing models during his hospitalization in Saint-Rémy, Vincent made color copies of other artists' works: he was especially fond of engravings and black-and-white sketches. He compared these adaptations to musical interpretations, and he explained his technique in a letter: "I take the black and white of Delacroix or Millet.... And then I improvise in color. This is not altogether my own, I am searching for memories of *their* pictures, but the memory, 'the vague consonance of colors which are at least right in feeling' are my own interpretation...I find that it teaches me things, and above all it sometimes gives me consolation." Adapting themes from the masters was Vincent's way of expressing his own feelings and thoughts. He saw his predecessors as his brothers, an emotionally charged word for him. While living in The Hague, van Gogh had gathered a large number of engravings. In particular, his collection featured some of Théodore Géricault's portraits of mental patients. Géricault was the first to look with an unflinching eye at the reality of the mentally ill, whom he saw not as an object of scorn, but as a fascinating, mysterious facet of life.

■ *The Drinkers* (after Daumier), 1890, The Art Institute of Chicago. Vincent's engraving collection included Daumier's *The Drinkers*. He reinterpreted this image highlighting the liveliness of the scene.

■ Théodore Géricault, *Woman Suffering from Obsessive Envy*, 1823, Musée des Beaux-Arts, Lyon. Géricault studied the effects of human passions on the face.

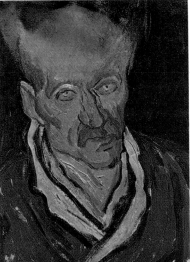

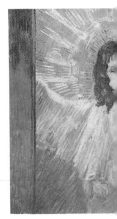

■ *Portrait of a Patient in Saint-Paul Hospital*, 1889, Van Gogh Museum, Amsterdam. This face seems to be the battleground for good and evil.

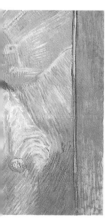

■ *Pietà* (after Delacroix), 1889, Van Gogh Museum, Amsterdam. As revealed by the red hair and beard, Christ's face is a self-portrait. The Virgin's blue robe is in stark contrast with the golden clouds, and her hands are the strong, solid hands of a worker.

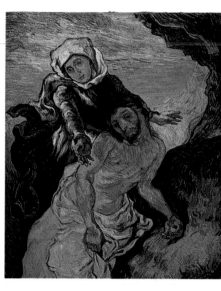

■ *Half-Figure of an Angel* (after Rembrandt), September 1889, location unknown. The ultimate objective of this painting seems to be the search of a blue suitable to Rembrandt. While the Dutch master had only used warm hues, Vincent gives this angel of light the breezy background of a spring sky. The face of the angel is not idealized, but full of sorrow and intense austerity.

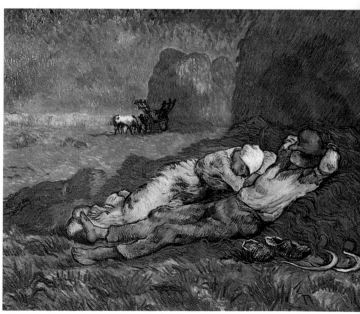

■ *Noon: Rest from Work* (after Millet), 1890, Musée d'Orsay, Paris. The relaxed intimacy of the figures may hint at the serenity of Theo's family life.

BACKGROUND

# In the shadow of *La Grande Dame*

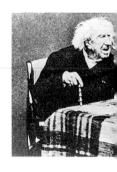

The French elections of 1889 had created a parliament with a republican majority. In the same year, in Paris, the Second International was created as a central organ connecting the different socialist movements. A new law was introduced that made military service compulsory for three years, not allowing for any exemption. The approaching end of the century meant that spiritualistic tendencies in literature and philosophy became even more deeply felt, while, from a technical and scientific point of view, great advances were made. "The current age is a critical moment: human thought is undergoing radical transformations. The ideas of the past are being shaken, but they are still very influential, while those that will replace them are still in the process of being formulated: that is why our time is a time of transformation and anarchy". This is how Gustave Le Bon described the *fin de siècle* in his work *The Psychology of Peoples*. Many artists signed a manifesto against the Eiffel Tower, saying: "We shall be forced to see the abominable shadow of this metallic column spread like an ink stain". Yet, from Robert Delaunay to Marc Chagall, the *Grande Dame* became the protagonist of many Parisian representations, such as *The Red Tower* or *La Ville de Paris*, created by Delaunay in 1911 and 1912 respectively.

■ This photograph shows the Eiffel Tower under construction. Erected between January 1867 and March 1889 by engineer Gustave Eiffel, for the Exposition Universelle, the *Grande Dame* of Paris weighs 7000 tons and is 300 meters (984 feet) high.

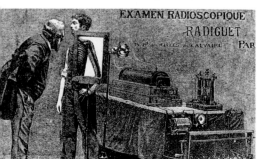

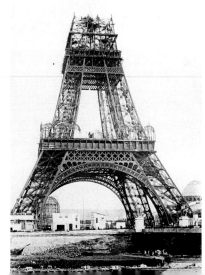

■ Discovered by Röntgen in 1895, the X-ray was just one of the many medical advances made at the turn of the century. This picture from *Parisien de Paris* shows an early radioscope.

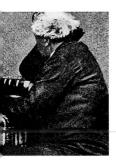

■ This was the first photograph taken by Nadar on August 30, 1886. The development of photography had profound consequences on contemporary painting. It also led to new studies being carried out in optical science.

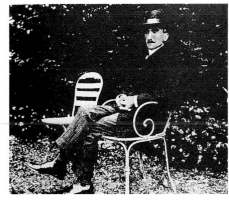

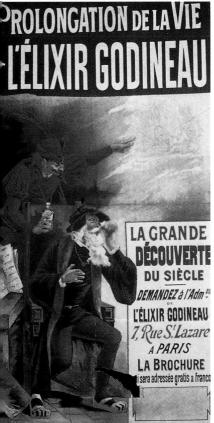

■ Pictured above, Henri-Louis Bergson (1859–1941) provided the most original reaction to the Positivism of Comte and Taine. His *Essay on the Immediate Data of Consciousness* (1889) was the first step towards affirming the supremacy of intuition over analytical reason.

■ Dust jacket of *Seven Princesses* by Maurice Maeterlinck. A leading Symbolist playwright and poet, Maeterlinck created many lyrical dramas, such as *Pelléas et Mélisande*, which was turned into an opera by Claude Debussy, and the allegorical fantasy *The Blue Bird*.

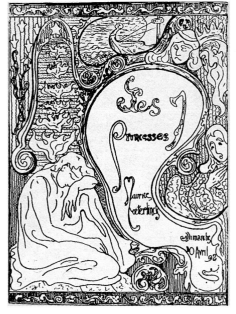

■ Above is an 1894 advertisement. Although hygiene was the main concept of the new medicine, charlatans and elixirs continued to exercise their fascination on people. Gustave Flaubert, in *Dictionary of Common Places*, wrote: "Too much health can be the cause of illness".

**1889**

# Pine Trees and Dandelions

After the last and longest period in the hospital of Saint-Rémy, from mid-February to the end of April 1890, van Gogh seemed to improve rapidly, and he completed this magnificent landscape kept at the Kröller-Müller Museum in Otterlo.

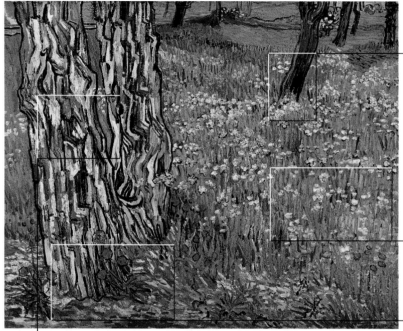

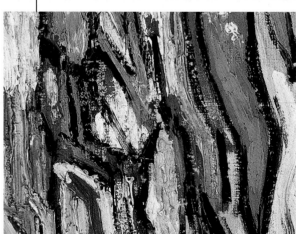

■ The complex chromaticism of the trunks includes strokes of lilac, blue, and orange. When seen from a distance, however, the image created is one of great verisimilitude. Vincent managed to convey even the feeling of roughness of the bark.

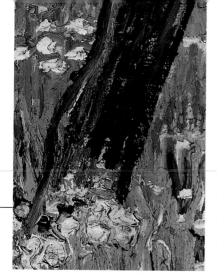

■ In a letter, Vincent commented that this painting seemed to him particularly eloquent and strong. While in the hospital of Saint-Rémy, Vincent's art changed considerably. By placing himself at the center of nature, he became more responsive to natural forms and colors. The intense colors of Arles were replaced by a more subtle palette and a greater attention to space and shapes.

■ The delicate green of the grass is achieved by a careful combination on canvas of blues and yellows. In this unusual painting, the visual field is restricted to the ground: the horizon has disappeared off the upper edge of the canvas. Later, Egon Schiele, Gustav Klimt, and other Expressionist artists followed in Vincent's footsteps, creating paintings that portrayed not the tree trunks, but the earth, where life begins.

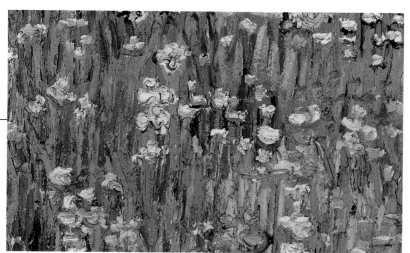

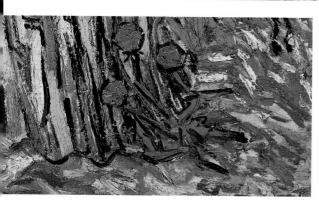

■ Vincent created a contrast between the gnarled tree trunks and the tender blades of grass. The delicate flowers seem to lean against the trees, searching for protection.

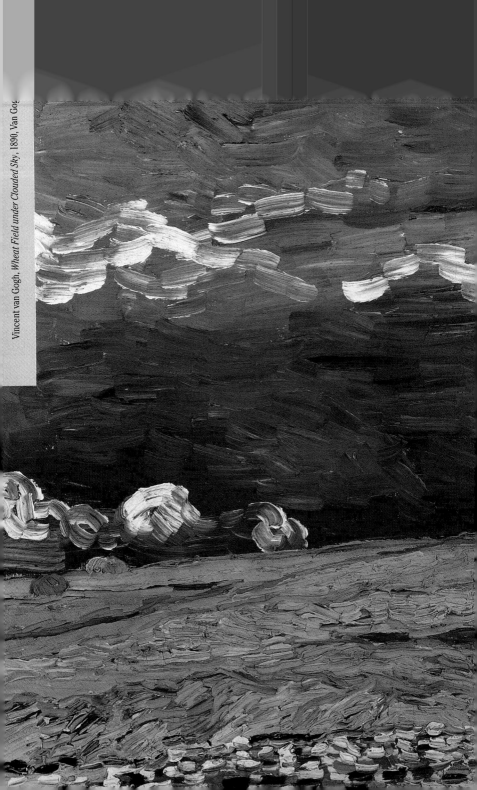

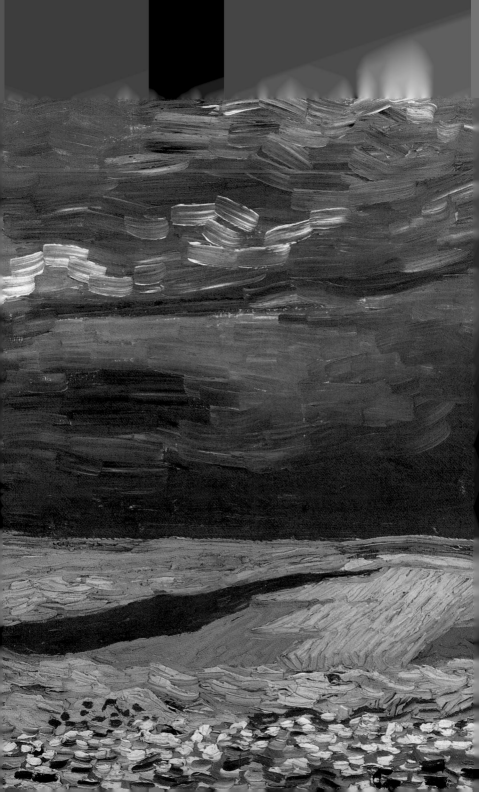

# La Belle Époque

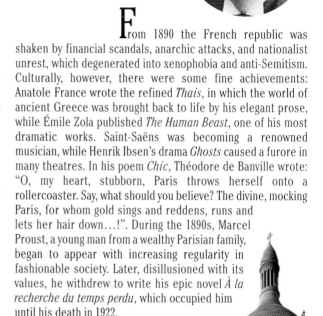

■ Right, Octave Mirbeau, writer and journalist, supported modern art against the past glories honored by the Académie. He wrote an article about van Gogh in *L'Écho de Paris* in which he stated: "Not only had he identified with nature, he had absorbed nature within himself. He selflessly passed his own life blood and sap onto the trees, skies, flowers, and fields that he painted".

■ A famous art dealer, Paul Durand-Ruel was the first to realize the importance of Impressionism and, in the window of his gallery in rue Neuve, he often exhibited works by Monet and Pissarro. He sold many Impressionist paintings to art collectors in Russia and the United States.

From 1890 the French republic was shaken by financial scandals, anarchic attacks, and nationalist unrest, which degenerated into xenophobia and anti-Semitism. Culturally, however, there were some fine achievements: Anatole France wrote the refined *Thais*, in which the world of ancient Greece was brought back to life by his elegant prose, while Émile Zola published *The Human Beast*, one of his most dramatic works. Saint-Saëns was becoming a renowned musician, while Henrik Ibsen's drama *Ghosts* caused a furore in many theatres. In his poem *Chic*, Théodore de Banville wrote: "O, my heart, stubborn, Paris throws herself onto a rollercoaster. Say, what should you believe? The divine, mocking Paris, for whom gold sings and reddens, runs and lets her hair down…!". During the 1890s, Marcel Proust, a young man from a wealthy Parisian family, began to appear with increasing regularity in fashionable society. Later, disillusioned with its values, he withdrew to write his epic novel *À la recherche du temps perdu*, which occupied him until his death in 1922.

■ The church of the Sacre-Cœur, started in 1873 and completed in 1919, is the symbol of Montmartre. It is a majestic building in the Romanesque-Byzantine style.

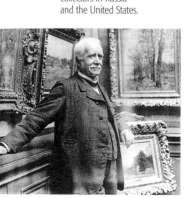

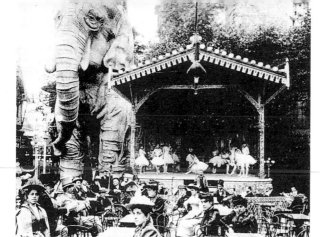

■ A colossal elephant erected specifically for the Exposition Universelle decorated the garden of the Moulin Rouge. Indoors, the beautiful belly dancer Zelaska performed her show.

■ Henri de Toulouse-Lautrec, *At the Moulin Rouge: The Dance*, 1890, Henry P. McIlhenny Collection, Philadelphia. Toulouse-Lautrec was the greatest interpreter of the Belle Époque. Without any moral judgment, he created joyful portraits of the great spectacle of Parisian night life.

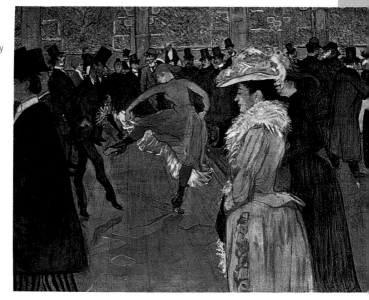

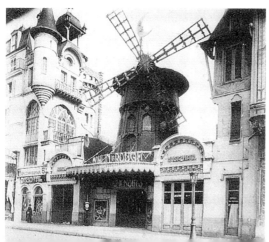

■ The Moulin Rouge, opened in 1889, is still the most famous cabaret in the world. It was the birthplace of the French *Can Can*. Here, you could see famous dancers such as La Goulue, Jane Avril, and May Milton.

121

**1890**

# The Church at Auvers

With this painting, now in the Musée d'Orsay in Paris, van Gogh conveys his inner torment: the building rises against a rich cobalt blue sky, and is rendered without any corners or straight lines.

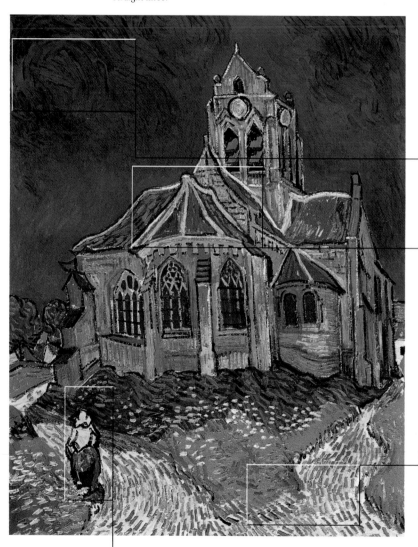

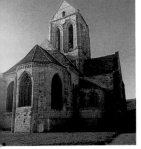

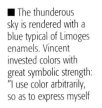

■ The thunderous sky is rendered with a blue typical of Limoges enamels. Vincent invested colors with great symbolic strength: "I use color arbitrarily, so as to express myself more forcibly". The sky seems to have invaded everything on earth: it even emanates from the windows of the church.

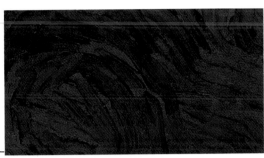

■ The transept and the chancel of the church of Auvers date back to the 12th century, while the large central tower was built a few decades later. "The roof is purple and partly orange", wrote Vincent. Van Gogh's funeral passed in front of this church.

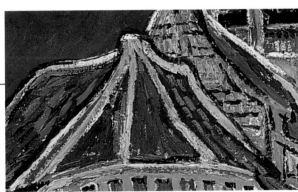

■ Van Gogh rendered the architectonic element of the chevet with soft, fluid lines. The building does not rise into the sky with determination, but it seems to quiver and reflect the artist's *pathos*.

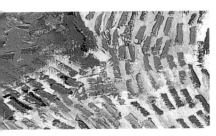

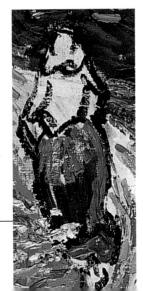

■ In his last sorrowful months, Vincent often thought of his homeland. His nostalgic feelings were so strong that the lonely woman portrayed from the back seems to belong in a Dutch painting and the church recalls an earlier image of the church at Nuenen (1884, Van Gogh Museum, Amsterdam).

■ Vincent often used the device of diverging paths to underpin a central subject. Here, rapid dashes of paint are used to indicate the direction of the paths, which surround the church.

# Doctor Saffron

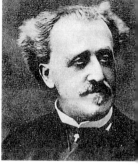

W̶hen he first arrived in Paris as a medical student in 1848, Paul Gachet, became friendly with a group of Realist artists. He soon started painting and engraving in his spare time and, when he taught artistic anatomy in 1875, the young Seurat was one of his students. In 1872 Gachet bought a house at Auvers-sur-Oise. Here he created a little studio, where he often entertained his artist friends, among whom were Cézanne and Guillaumin. He also started to collect their works. He had several artists in his care, including Pissarro and Renoir. An expert on mental disorders, he had written a thesis on melancholy, and was Theo's first choice when he was looking for a doctor for his brother. At first Vincent thought that Gachet was an eccentric man, but the two established a rapport of mutual understanding. A new, welcoming friend, eager to discuss art with him, did Vincent good. He created two paintings of Gachet, portraying him "with a white cap, his hands paler than his face, a blue jacket, and a cobalt blue background". Gachet's yellow hair earned him the nickname Doctor Saffron.

■ Born in Lille, and therefore a northern man, like Vincent, Paul Ferdinand Gachet was a student of homeopathic doctor Vincent Simon, one of Chopin's last physicians. An amateur painter and engraver, he signed his works with the pseudonym van Rijssel. He died on January 9, 1909.

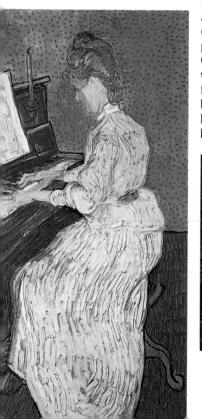

■ *Marguerite Gachet at the Piano*, June 1890, Kunstmuseum, Basel. Vincent wrote of the difficulties encountered while creating this portrait of Gachet's 19-year-old daughter. The pink dress is complemented by the green background.

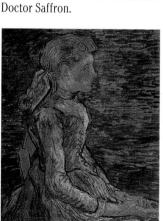

■ *Portrait of Adeline Ravoux*, June 1890, Private Collection, Switzerland. Adeline Ravoux was the daughter of the owner of the inn where van Gogh stayed during his months at Auvers. The serious profile and simple demeanor are reminiscent of 15th-century Italian portraits.

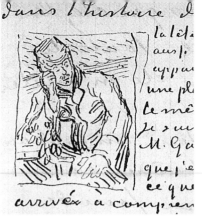

■ This letter contains a sketch of Gachet. Among the works the doctor owned was a female nude by Guillaumin. Upon seeing that this painting had not yet been framed, Vincent asked Gachet to rectify the injustice. When the doctor failed to comply, Vincent threatened him with a gun.

■ *Portrait of Doctor Gachet*, 1890, Musée d'Orsay, Paris. The foxgloves (*Digitalis*) on the table represent the doctor's profession. His pose is inspired by the traditional iconography of the melancholic temperament. The soft, sinuous lines seem to reflect the pathetic bent of the man.

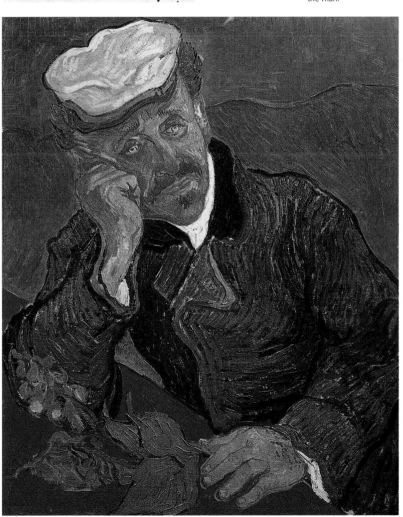

**1890**

# The last journey

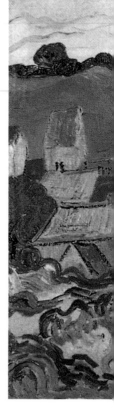

Worried by the news from Saint-Rémy, Theo invited Vincent to Paris. His wife Jo had given birth to a son, whom they named after Vincent. Enamoured of his nephew, Vincent expressed the wish that he should "have a soul less unquiet than mine, which is foundering…". On May 21, after just three days in Paris, Vincent went to Auvers-sur-Oise where he received care from Doctor Gachet. He worked hard, and anxiously awaited Theo's visits. However, Theo was plagued by health and work problems and, unable to go to Auvers, asked his brother to go to the capital. Things did not improve and eventually Theo was forced to cancel the holidays he had planned with Vincent. Feeling deserted, Vincent's bouts of self-destruction resumed.

On July 23, he wrote: "This misery will never end". On July 27, he wandered into the fields with a gun and shot himself: the bullet, aimed at the heart, was deflected by the diaphragm. He returned to his room, where the extent of his injury was soon revealed. Vincent van Gogh died on July 29. His brother Theo died six months later, on January 25, 1891.

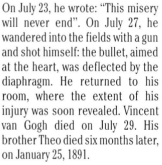

■ Auvers is a quiet village in Val-d'Oise, about 30 kilometers (18 miles) from Paris. It lies near the l'Isle-Adam, on the ridge overlooking the river Oise.

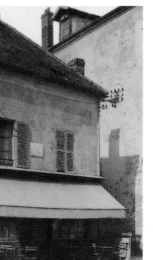

■ The humble room where Vincent spent the last few months of his life was above the café owned by the Ravoux family. Vincent's room looked onto the town hall.

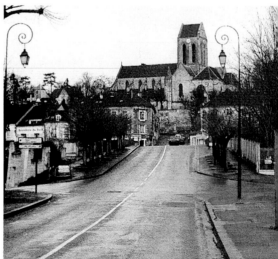

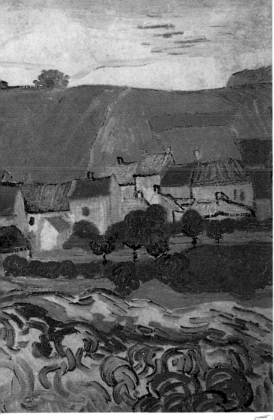

■ *View of Auvers*, 1890, Van Gogh Museum, Amsterdam. Auvers is surrounded by green meadows and wheat fields. The landscape painter Charles-François Daubigny had a studio in Auvers, and Honoré Daumier spent his final years in the nearby village of Valmondois.

■ *Houses at Auvers with a Peasant Walking*, 1890, Van Gogh Museum, Amsterdam.

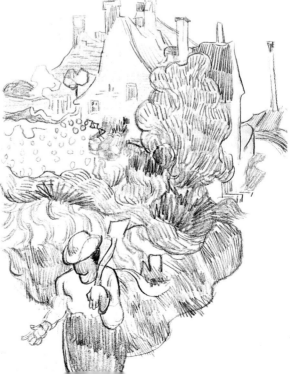

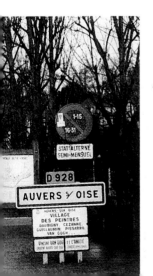

# Wheat Field with Crows

"I hear the wings of the crows beat like cymbals above the fields. It is as if the rising tide was becoming unbearable for van Gogh". Thus wrote Antonin Artaud about this painting, now in the Van Gogh Museum in Amsterdam.

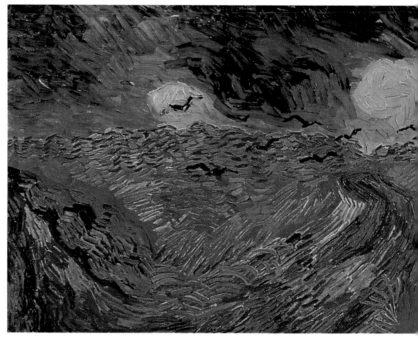

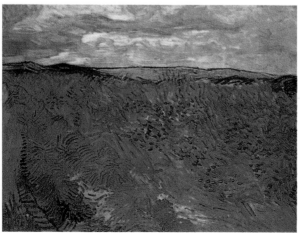

■ *Wheat Field with Cornflowers*, July 1890, Private Collection. "They are vast fields of wheat under troubled skies, and I did not need to go out of my way to express sadness and extreme loneliness". Vincent's last landscapes symbolize the end of Impressionism: while Monet's fields had a lively, reassuring palette, van Gogh's vast plains resemble biblical landscapes awaiting the last judgment.

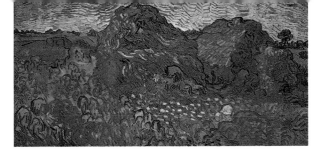

■ *Field with Wheat Stacks*, 1890, Hahnloser Collection, Bern. The field is created with swirling, horseshoe-shaped lines. These brushstrokes influenced the Fauves.

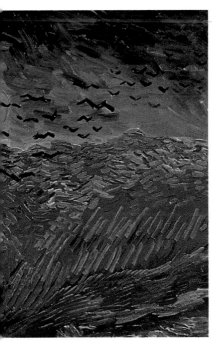

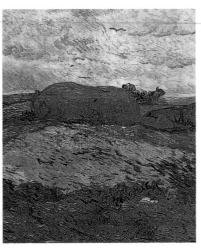

■ *Haystacks under a Rainy Sky*, 1890, Kröller-Müller Museum, Otterlo. In this painting, the recurring image of the crows, figures of destiny, stands out against the bright masses of color. "After the harvest I sometimes sigh, and think of when I myself will be part of nature and will create something with my art".

■ *Wheat Field under Clouded Sky*, July 1890, Carnegie Institute, Pittsburgh. The direction of the brushstrokes helps to convey the irregular shape and texture of the fields. They are of "a delicate yellow, with the regular speck of the green of flowering potato plants, under a sky of delicate tones of blue, white, pink and violet". This detailed description of the colors indicates Vincent's desire to create a serene painting.

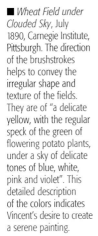

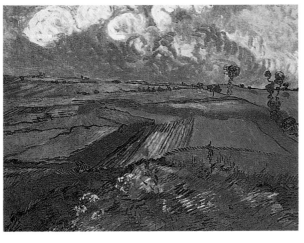

**1890**

# After Vincent

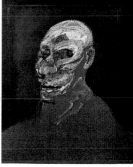

V incent van Gogh's works caused a sensation in the artistic world of the early 20th century, especially in Germany. Many artists came to realize that van Gogh's richly charged colors and fluid shapes could bring life and soul to an art that late Impressionism was making increasingly sterile. Reacting against the critically acclaimed realistic images of this period, some young painters joined in a movement called *Die Brücke*, "The Bridge". Founded in Dresden in 1905, this group believed that Vincent's artistic language was the perfect means of conveying the romantic tension within them and their tendency to express rather than represent. This movement eventually developed into Expressionism. Van Gogh became a model for those artists who, feeling that the exterior world should be the expression of their emotional state, wanted to portray the sense of contemporary uneasiness. Their art was not a consolation but a disturbing provocation to denounce the "whitened sepulchres" of the bourgeoisie. Vincent's heritage, the deepest sense of his work, moved beyond the issues of painting and literature to become a meditation on the rapport between art and life.

■ Francis Bacon, *Head of a Man: Study of a Drawing by van Gogh*, 1959, Private Collection. An ingenious 20th-century painter, Francis Bacon was heavily influenced by Vincent's self-portraits, which he distorted into grotesque masks.

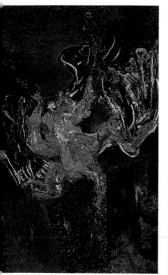

■ Chaim Soutine, *Dead Fowl (Rooster)*, 1926, The Art Institute of Chicago. Soutine's thick application of color is clearly influenced by van Gogh.

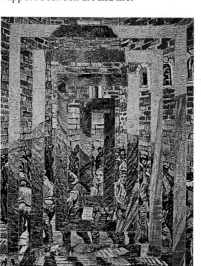

■ Jirí Kolář, *The Labyrinth*, 1952. The Bohemian artist Kolář created this maze-like structure as a homage to Vincent.

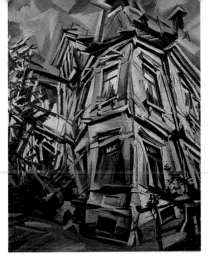

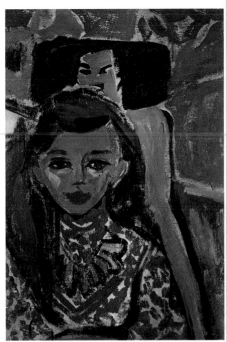

■ Ludwig Meidner, *The House on the Corner*, 1913, Thyssen-Bornemisza Collection, Madrid. In this work, colors represent both soul and nature.

■ Ernst Ludwig Kirchner, *Portrait of Fränzi in Front of Carved Stool*, 1910, Thyssen-Bornemisza Collection, Madrid.

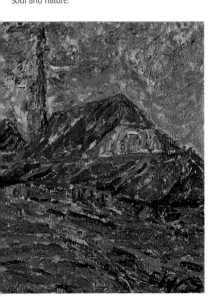

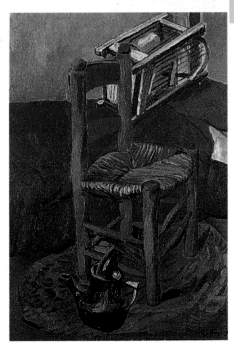

■ Erich Heckel, *Brick Factory in Dangast*, 1907, Thyssen-Bornemisza Collection, Madrid.

■ Renato Guttuso, *Interior with Cage*, 1939, Private Collection. Guttuso reworked van Gogh 's chair, portraying it with heartfelt anxiety.

**1890**

# The legend of van Gogh

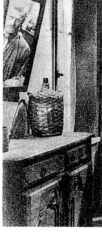

Van Gogh was a contradictory man who lived his life divided between a profound need for love and his arrogant shyness, between his methodic self-destruction carried out in cafés and brothels and the proud awareness of his value as an painter. He is one of the best examples of the "doomed" artist. However, too often critics have failed to take into consideration van Gogh's extremely lucid accounts of his works to define him exclusively as a man of passions and instinct. As it is often the case with exceptionally creative characters, the media has become interested in his life, turning it into a romantic and cathartic tale of art and madness. Many great film directors of our time have tried to portray Vincent's life and art: not only Vincente Minnelli in his famous *Lust for Life*, but also Robert Altman, Maurice Pialat, and Alain Resnais. Philosopher Karl Jaspers dedicated a chapter in his essay *Genius and Madness* to Vincent, comparing him with other artists such as Johan August Strindberg and Johann Christian Friedrich Hölderlin, and underlining the coexistence in van Gogh's personality of lucidity and insanity.

■ Above is a still from *Lust for Life*. Director Vincente Minnelli gave the objects in the room the same location they had in van Gogh's paintings. Moving from the musical genre to a serious biography marked Minnelli's coming of age.

■ Below are Martin Scorsese and Akira Terao in a scene from Akira Kurosawa's 1990 film *Dreams*. In the film, a tragic Vincent narrates Japanese tales on great masters who died for their art.

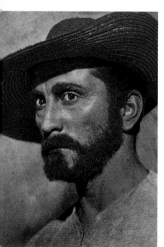

■ Above is Kirk Douglas in scene from the 1956 film *Lust for Life* by Vincente Minnelli. In the movie, based on Irving Stone's novel, Douglas portrayed Vincent as a neurotic, difficult character.

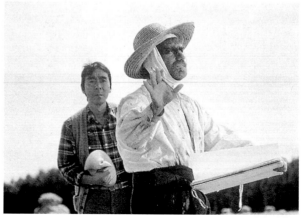

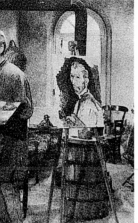

■ Antonin Artaud, *Self-Portrait*, 1946. The thin, spirited Artaud, with his anarchically long hair, represents himself with a bandaged ear, in memory of Vincent. According to Artaud, author of violently expressionist theatrical pieces, Doctor Gachet led van Gogh to suicide on behalf of society.

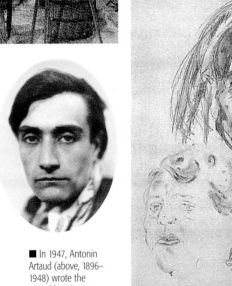

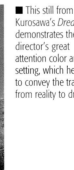

■ In 1947, Antonin Artaud (above, 1896–1948) wrote the pamphlet *Vincent van Gogh, Suicide by Society*.

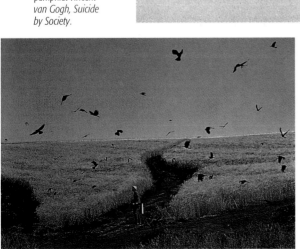

■ This still from Akira Kurosawa's *Dreams* demonstrates the director's great attention color and setting, which helped to convey the transition from reality to dream.

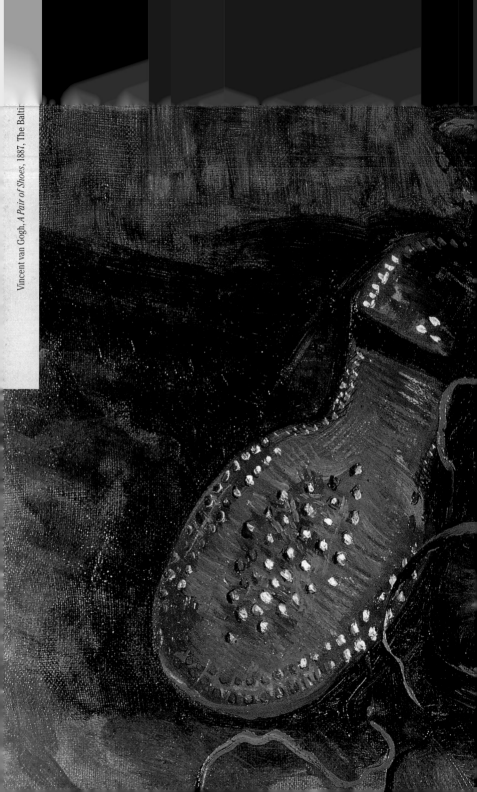

# Index

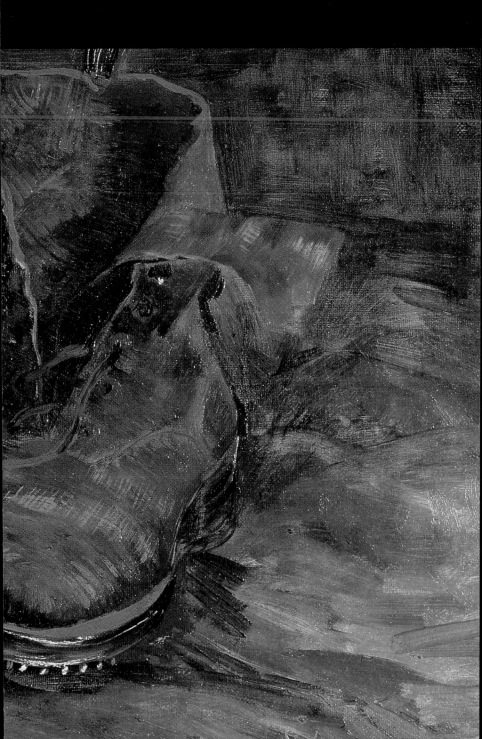

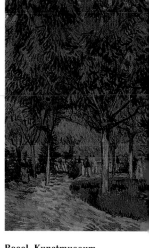

■ *A Lane in the*
*Public Garden at Arles,*
1888, Kröller-Müller
Museum, Otterlo.

## Note

*The places listed in this section*
*refer to the current location of*
*van Gogh's works. Where more*
*than one work is housed in the*
*same* **place***, they are listed*
*in chronological order.*

### Amsterdam, Stedelijk Museum
*Vegetable Gardens in Montmartre*,
pp. 38–39.

### Amsterdam, Van Gogh Museum
*The Sower*, p. 25;
*Still Life with Cabbage and Clogs*,
pp. 6–7;
*The State Lottery Office*, p. 26;
*Beach at Scheveningen in*
*Stormy Weather*, p. 26;
*Still Life with Open Bible,*
*Candlestick, and Novel*, p. 19;
*The Old Cemetery Tower*

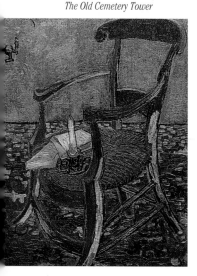

*at Neunen*, p. 28;
*Peasant Woman*, pp. 32–33;
*The Potato Eaters*, pp. 36–37;
*Vegetable Gardens in*
*Montmartre*, p. 49;
*Le Tambourin*, pp. 44–45;
*Bridge in the Rain*, p. 53;
*Japonaiserie: Oiran*, p. 53;
*Self-Portrait with Felt Hat*, p. 2;
*Self-Portrait with the Easel*, p. 54;
*The White Orchard*, p. 63;
*The Pink Orchard*, pp. 62–63;
*Blossoming Pear Tree*, p. 63;
*Peach Trees in Blossom*, p. 63;
*The Zouave*, p. 75;
*Harvest at La Crau, with*
*Montmajour in the Background*,
p. 74;
*View of Arles with Irises in*
*the Foreground*, pp. 60–61;
*Still Life: Vase with Fourteen*
*Sunflowers*, p. 95;
*The Artist's Bedroom*, p. 70;
*Two White Butterflies*, pp. 94–95;
*Fountain in the Garden of*
*Saint-Paul Hospital*, p. 101;
*Still Life with Irises*, pp. 102–03;
*Pietà*, p. 113;
*Portrait of a Patient in Saint-Paul*
*Hospital*, p. 112;
*Study of Cuckoo-Pints*, p. 94;
*Wheat Field with Cypresses*, p. 104;
*Wheat Field with Crows*,
pp. 128–29;
*Wheat Field under Clouded Sky*,
pp. 118–19;
*Houses at Auvers with a Peasant*
*Walking*, p. 127;
*View of Auvers*, pp. 126–27.

### Baltimore, The Baltimore Museum of Art
*A Pair of Shoes*, pp. 134–35.

■ *Paul Gauguin's*
*Armchair*, 1888, Van Gogh
Museum, Amsterdam.

### Basel, Kunstmuseum
*View of Paris from Montmartre*,
p. 41;
*Marguerite Gachet at the Piano*,
p. 124.

### Bern, Hahnloser Collection
*Field with Wheat Stacks*, p. 129.

### Boston, Museum of Fine Arts
*Portrait of Joseph Roulin*,
p. 73.

### Brussels, Musée d'Art Moderne
*Seascape at Saintes-Maries-de-*
*la-Mer*, p. 85.

### Budapest, Szépmüvészeti Múzeum
*Woman Churning Milk*, p. 30.

### Buffalo, Albright-Knox Art Gallery
*The Old Mill*, p. 79.

### Chicago, The Art Institute of Chicago
*Vincent's Bedroom*, p. 71;
*Public Park with Weeping Willow:*
*The Poet's Garden I*, p. 79;
*The Drinkers*, pp. 112–13.

### Cleveland, The Cleveland Museum of Art
*The Road Menders*, p. 104.

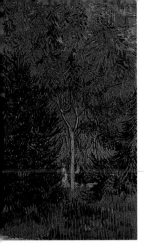

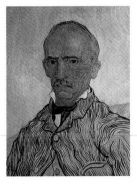

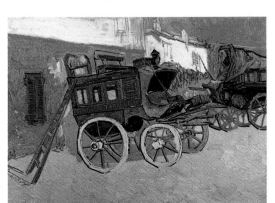

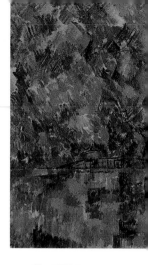

## Note

*All the names mentioned here are artists, intellectuals, politicians, and businessmen who had some connection with van Gogh, as well as painters, sculptors, and architects who were contemporaries or active in the same places as van Gogh.*

**Bernard, Émile** (Lille, 1868 – Paris, 1941), French painter and writer. He worked in Pont-Aven with Paul Gauguin and Paul Sérusier. In 1893 he published Vincent's letters, pp. 60, 63, 68, 85, 87, 96–97.

**Bing, Samuel**, art dealer and founder of the magazine *Le Japon illustré*. Van Gogh purchased several Japanese prints from him, p. 52.

**Boch, Anna**, sister of the Belgian artist Eugène Boch, she purchased Vincent van Gogh's *The Red Vineyard* for 400 francs. Today the work is housed in the Pushkin Museum in Moscow, p. 67.

**Boch, Eugène**, Belgian artist and poet who posed for van Gogh. Vincent thought that "this young man who resembles Dante" was an excellent model, pp. 66–67.

**Breitner, George Hendrik** (Rotterdam, 1857 – Amsterdam, 1923), Dutch painter influenced by the Hague School, particularly Maris and Mesdag. His preferred subjects were landscapes, daily scenes, and common people, pp. 16, 23.

**Bruegel, Pieter the Elder** (Breughel, c.1528 – Brussels, 1569), Flemish painter. Influenced by Bosch, he gave a new lease of life to the traditional northern landscape, which he portrayed in a popular, simple way, pp. 34–35.

**Carbentus, Anna Cornelia** (1819–1907), Vincent van Gogh's mother, pp. 8–9.

**Carbentus, Jet**, daughter of one of Vincent van Gogh's great-aunts. She married the painter Anton Mauve, p. 17.

**Carbentus, Sophy**, Vincent van Gogh's great-aunt. The artist stayed with her during his time in The Hague, p. 16.

**Cézanne, Paul** (Aix-en-Provence, 1839–1906), French painter. Initially associated with Impressionism, he became increasingly committed to the study of form and structure, pp. 54, 80–81, 101, 126.

**Constable, John** (East Bergholt, 1776 – London, 1837), English landscape artist. Influenced by the Dutch masters, he sought to render scenery as realistically as possible. Using touches of pure white and other vibrant colors, he perfectly conveyed the changing effects of light, pp. 18–19.

**Cormon, Fernand** (Paris, 1845–1924), Fernand-Anne Piestre, also known as Cormon, French painter. He was a careful illustrator of working life in the country and the city, pp. 40, 96.

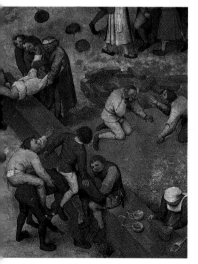

■ Pieter Bruegel the Elder, *Children's Games*, 1559, Kunsthistorisches Museum, Vienna.

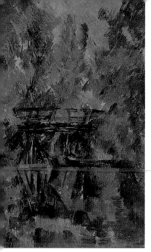

■ Paul Cézanne,
*Bridge over the
Pond*, 1898, Pushkin
Museum, Moscow.

■ Gustave Courbet,
*The Peasants of Flagey
Returning from the Fair*,
1855, Musée des Beaux-
Arts, Besançon.

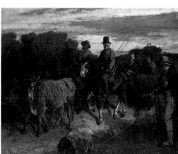

**Costa, Mendes da**, young
professor of Jewish origins. He
taught Vincent van Gogh when the
artist was studying Protestant
theology at the University of
Amsterdam, p. 22.

**Courbet, Gustave** (Ornans,
1819 – La Tour de Peilz, 1877),
French painter. Leader of the
Realist school, he rebelled
against the Académie by depicting
scenes from everyday life, p. 34.

**Daudet, Alphonse** (Nîmes,
1840 – Paris, 1897), French writer,
noted for his humorous tales of
Provençal life, pp. 74, 86.

**Daumier, Honoré**
(Marseille, 1808 – Valmondois,
1879), French caricaturist,
painter, and sculptor. Best known
for for his lithographs, which are
imbued with political satire and
social criticism, Daumier also

produced paintings and sculptures
after 1860, pp. 18, 35, 112, 121, 127.

**Delacroix, Eugène** (Carenton-
Saint-Maurice, 1798 – Paris, 1863),
French painter. He illustrated
several important events of his
time as well as creating literary,
exotic, and historical paintings.
The epitome of Romantic art, his
work is characterized by brilliant
colors and expressive freedom,
pp. 30, 112–113.

**Dickens, Charles**
(Landport, Portsmouth, 1812 –
Gad's Hill, Rochester, 1870),
English writer. Dickens was a
prolific writer, who through his
sympathetic and humorous
novels expressed his social and
humanitarian concerns, pp. 18–19.

**Doré, Gustave** (Strasbourg,
1832 – Paris, 1883), French
illustrator and engraver. He was
famous for his illustrations to
such books as Dante's *Inferno*,
*Don Quixote*, and the Bible. He
also created many humorous
prints as well as works of social
criticism, pp. 18, 110–11.

**Dostoyevsky, Fyodor**
(Moscow, 1821 – St. Petersburg,

1881), Russian writer. His satiric,
naturalist style is combined
with a great compassion for
human suffering, pp. 24, 104.

**Escalier, Patience**, peasant,
portrayed by van Gogh in 1888,
p. 67.

**Fildes, Luke** (Liverpool, 1844 –
London, 1927), English engraver
whose illustrations are imbued
with social realism, pp. 18–19.

**Gachet, Marguerite**, daughter
of Doctor Paul Gachet, portrayed
by van Gogh in 1890, p. 126.

**Gachet, Paul Ferdinand**,
homeopathic doctor, amateur
artist, and collector. He treated
Vincent van Gogh at Auvers,
pp. 120, 126–27, 131.

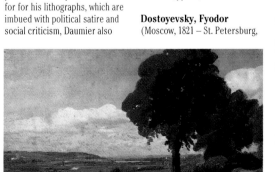

■ John Constable,
*A Lane at East Bergholt*,
1809, Victoria and Albert
Museum, London.

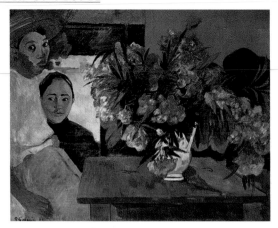

■ Paul Gauguin,
*Te Tirae Farani*
(*The Flowers of
France*), 1891, Pushkin
Museum, Moscow.

**Gauguin, Paul** (Paris, 1848 –
Atuona, 1903), French Post-
Impressionist artist. Founder
of the Pont-Aven School, he
contributed to the creation of
Synthetism and Symbolism, in
which real and visionary elements
were combined and color was
freed from its representational
function. Inspired by primitive
art and Japanese prints, his work
is characterized by areas of pure,
flat color, pp. 27, 46, 50, 56, 65,
68–69, 86–87, 92, 96–97.

**Géricault, Théodore**
(Rouen, 1791 – Paris, 1824),
French painter influenced by
the work of Michelangelo. His
work is characterized by great
romanticism and vitality, p. 112.

**Ginoux, Joseph**, owner of
the Café de la Gare, beneath the
"Yellow House" at Arles. Vincent
van Gogh lived here in 1888, p. 60.

**Ginoux, Marie**, wife of Joseph
Ginoux. Van Gogh portrayed her

several times with the typical
Arlesian dress, pp. 60, 86–87.

**Groot, Gordina de**, peasant
portrayed by van Gogh in his
paintings *Peasant Woman* and
*The Potato Eaters*, p. 33.

**Hiroshige, Ando** (Edo,
modern Tokyo, 1797–1858),
Japanese artist who created many
*Ukiyo-e* prints. His views of the
country around Kyoto and Lake
Biwa are remarkable, pp. 52–53.

**Hokusai, Katsushika**
(Edo, modern Tokyo, 1760–
1849), Japanese painter and
engraver, master of *Ukiyo-e*. His
vigorous calligraphic virtuosity,
evident in his landscapes and
everyday scenes, influenced the
French Impressionists, pp. 52, 81.

**Hoornik, Christine (Sien)**,
portrayed many times by Vincent
van Gogh. She had a relationship
with Vincent during his stay in
The Hague, pp. 26–27.

**Hugo, Victor** (Besançon,
1802 – Paris, 1885), French poet,
novelist, and dramatist. A
leading French Romantic, his
opus includes poems, historical
novels, political writings, and
novels with a humanitarian
message, pp. 19, 40–41, 69.

**Israëls, Joszef** (Groningen,
1824 – The Hague, 1911), Dutch
painter. One of the leading
members of the Hague School,
he is best known for his scenes
of peasants and fishermen, p. 16.

**Kempis, Thomas à** (Kempen,
c.1380 – Agnetenberg, 1471),
German writer and ascetic. He
is remembered for his mystic
pamphlets and devotional
writings, p. 22.

**Loyer, Eugenie**, daughter of
Vincent's landlady. The artist fell
in love with her while he was in
London. In the letters to his
brother Theo, he referred to
her as Ursula, pp. 18, 27.

**Maris, Jacob Hendricus**
(The Hague, 1837 – Karlsbad,
1899), Dutch painter and engraver.

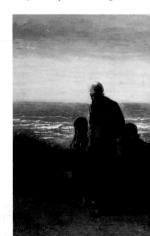

■ Jean-François Millet, *The Sheepfold by Moonlight*, 1861, Musée d'Orsay, Paris.

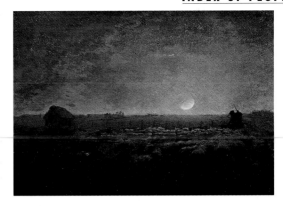

Influenced by the French Realists, he was a leading member of the Hague School, p. 16.

**Maris, Matthijs, known as Matthias** (The Hague, 1839 – London, 1917), Dutch painter, brother of Jacob, and a member of the Hague School. His urban landscapes were influenced by English Pre-Raphaelite art, p. 16.

**Matisse, Henri** (Le Cateau, 1869 – Cimiez, 1954), French painter and sculptor. Initially influenced by Impressionism, he later experimented with pointillist techniques before developing the vividly contrasting colors associated with the Fauves. He always maintained his own style, however, and his works are characterized by a bright coloring and a fluid lines, pp. 40, 43, 83.

**Mauve, Anton** (Zaandam, 1838 – Arnhem, 1888), Dutch painter. Influenced by Corot, Millet, and the Dutch tradition, he was part of the Hague School with the Maris bothers and Joszef Israëls. His landscapes served as models for the young Vincent pp. 16, 26.

**Millet, Jean-François** (Gruchy, 1814 – Barbizon, 1875), French painter. Closer to Romanticism than to Realism, he offered a serious, often melancholic image of work and life in the country, pp. 25, 30–31, 112–13.

**Milliet, Paul-Eugène**, Second Lieutenant of the Zouaves, he befriended van Gogh, who painted his portrait in 1888, p. 67.

**Mistral, Frédéric** (Maillane, 1830–1914), French Provençal poet. He contributed to the revival of Provençal language and literature, pp. 74, 84–85.

**Monet, Claude** (Paris, 1840 – Giverny, 1926), French painter. The quintessential Impressionist, he tried to portray on canvas the most ethereal things, such as the changing effects of light. He was devoted to painting *en plein*

*air* and even had a studio boat built, the better to observe nature. His dedication to Impressionist principles never faltered throughout his long career, pp. 40, 52, 56, 122.

**Monticelli, Adolphe** (Marseille, 1824–86), French painter of Italian origin. Heavily influenced by the Romantic pictorial tradition, his paintings anticipated the Impressionists, pp. 56, 60, 75.

**Peyron, Doctor**, doctor in charge of the hospital of Saint-Paul-de-Mausole when van Gogh was admitted in May 1889, p. 100.

**Pissarro, Camille** (Saint-Thomas, 1830 – Paris, 1903), French painter. The only artist to exhibit works in all eight Impressionist shows, Pissarro is generally regarded as the father figure of the group. He briefly experimented with pointillist techniques and influenced many Post-Impressionists, pp. 46–47, 50, 56, 68, 122, 126.

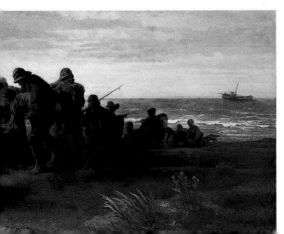

■ Joszef Israëls, *The Drowned Fisherman*, 1861, National Gallery, London.

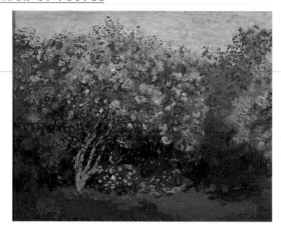

■ Claude Monet,
*Beneath the Lilacs*,
1873, Pushkin
Museum, Moscow.

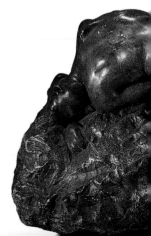

■ Paul Signac, *In a Time of Harmony*, 1895, Pushkin Museum, Moscow.

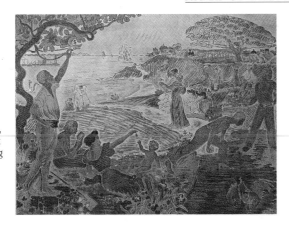

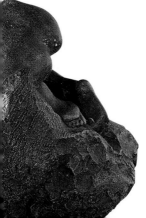

■ Auguste Rodin, *Danaë*, 1901, Private Collection.

# A DK PUBLISHING BOOK

Visit us on the World Wide Web at http://www.dk.com

TRANSLATOR
**Sylvia Tombesi-Walton**

DESIGN ASSISTANCE
Joanne Mitchell

EDITOR
Jo Marceau

MANAGING EDITOR
Anna Kruger

Series of monographs
edited by Stefano Peccatori and Stefano Zuffi

Text by Anna Torterolo

PICTURE SOURCES
Archivio Electa, Milan
Alinari-Giraudon, Florence
Elemond Editori Associati wishes to thank all those museums and
photographic libraries who have kindly supplied pictures, and would be pleased
to hear from copyright holders in the event of uncredited picture sources.

Project created in conjunction with
La Biblioteca editrice s.r.l., Milan

First published in the United States in 1999 by DK Publishing Inc.
95 Madison Avenue, New York, New York 10016

ISBN 0-7894-4143-8

Library of Congress Catalog Card Number: 98-86848

First published in Great Britain in 1999
by Dorling Kindersley Limited,
9 Henrietta Street, London WC2E 8PS

A CIP catalogue record of this book is available from the British Library.

ISBN 0751307289

2 4 6 8 10 9 7 5 3 1

Printed by Elemond s.p.a. at Martellago (Venice)